PREACHING
THROUGH THE
CHRISTIAN YEAR
6

PREACHING THROUGH THE CHRISTIAN YEAR

6

Sermon outlines for the seasons of the Church's year

Fenton Morley

MOWBRAYS

LONDON & OXFORD

© W. Fenton Morley 1977

ISBN 0 264 66401 9

First published in 1977
by A. R. Mowbray & Co. Ltd
Saint Thomas House,
Oxford, OX2 0EG

Text set in 12 13pt Monotype Bembo by Cotswold Typesetting Ltd., Gloucester
Printed in Great Britain by Lowe & Brydone Printers Limited, Thetford, Norfolk

PREFACE

A somewhat disgruntled churchman complained to his vicar that although he must have heard three thousand sermons, he could not remember any one of them. The vicar replied that his wife had cooked for him three thousand meals. He could not remember any of them, but he was sure that they had done him some good!

But, more seriously, every sermon can bear some fruit, if only to the man who preaches it; that is if, like most of us in the ministry, he preaches it in the first instance not to others or even against others—as some may fancy at times—but to himself. The vitality of his sermon depends on its relation to his own experience of God, his understanding of the needs of others, and his awareness of what is really happening in the Church and in the world. Moreover, in the pulpit as in every other realm of life, a man has to live with himself.

There is, however, another side to preaching. There are signs that the sermon is coming back into its own as a medium of teaching as well as of proclamation. More and more of the laity are asking for instruction from the pulpit, as also in group discussion, not as a dehydrated doctrinal diet but as a means of clarifying the issues of modern life and the relevance of the Gospel to them. So one main purpose of the sermon outlines which follow is, unashamedly, that of encouraging what might be called a theological view of life.

If there is another overall intention, it is that of drawing attention to the life-situation in which Jesus taught and the early Christians had to apply his teaching. Theirs was a missionary situation, and so is our own.

I should like to thank the many clergymen, ministers and others who have made use of my previous book, the fourth in this series, and have made helpful comments and critisisms of it. They include, not least, those who have told me that they have incorporated these outlines in their own sermons—and thus prevented my using them myself when I have visited their churches!

Finally, I gladly express my gratitude to my wife who has added to my indebtedness to her throughout our forty years together in marriage and ministry, by typing the manuscript of this book.

Salisbury 1977   *Fenton Morley*

CONTENTS

INTRODUCTION

What is required of me as Editor of this series of Sermon Outlines is not to introduce a writer, for Fenton Morley has already contributed a volume to this series; it is to introduce a book.

The regular preacher must have ideas. They are as basic for him as groceries are for the housewife. It is to be expected that he will have some ideas of his own, but unless he has an extremely fertile mind he will have insufficient to go on producing sermons week after week for a regular congregation. It is hard work. Let there be no misunderstanding. All too easily the food offered from the pulpit can be tasteless, stale, unnourishing stuff, deficient in vitamins. To avoid this the preacher will have to shop around until he finds goods suitable for his own particular ministry. So let me try to sell you Fenton Morley's new book of sermon outlines. It will be surprising if a great many preachers do not welcome it. Preachers need fresh ideas and they will find them on this counter.

What sort of ideas? For the most part so straightforward, even traditional, that the reader may reckon that he could have thought of them himself. But that is the point! We do not think of them *when we need them*. One reason, therefore, why this book will be useful to so many preachers is because there is nothing peculiar or odd about the material, nothing any normal preacher could not use himself, yes, and perhaps even improve on. The author will not quarrel with this suggestion.

In a sense the outlines here are quietly Anglican. (What would you expect from a Dean of a Cathedral?) Not simply because they follow the Church's year, nor because they draw out basic Christian truths as the Anglican Church has received them, but because they breathe an air of modesty, reserve, unobtrusive learning, and a pastoral aim. This preacher is out to teach people the Christian faith and the Christian way of life, to teach them in a modern world very different from yesterday's world. He is not out to parade his knowledge—

though the reader will pick up all sorts of unexpected bits of information such as the origin of pancakes, Valentines and Bank Holidays—he is out to bring Christ to people and people to Christ. This is as it should be. Fenton Morley preaches when he teaches and teaches when he preaches.

And he doesn't forget the preacher's biggest problem—how to offer a fresh word for the big Festivals and for Harvest and Remembrance Sunday. It is all here in this book. If exciting, and, dramatic stuff is what is required, this is not the place to find it, but if wholesome food with which to feed congregations, not too strong and not too weak, this is the volume to purchase and use. I wish it good success.

Lambeth Palace 1977   *D. W. Cleverley Ford*

ADVENT

Sing a new song

Few things can cause more controversy in a church than a proposal to change a hymn book. We may resent the use of new tunes to familiar words. We can be equally critical of verses which reflect modern problems. Some of us cling to the hymns we learned as children. Yet it may be questioned whether the enthusiasm with which we sing hymns is matched by genuine conviction as to the beliefs which they convey.

Archbishop William Temple put this question during a University Mission service at Oxford. His congregation was singing the hymn 'When I survey the wondrous Cross'. Just when they were about to sing the last verse, he stopped them. He asked them to read the words silently:

> 'Were the whole realm of nature mine,
> That were an offering far too small;
> Love so amazing, so divine,
> Demands my soul, my life, my all.'

Then they sang the verse, quietly and thoughtfully. It was the most moving incident of the entire mission.

1 Songs of the prophets

The Old Testament has many examples of people being called to think seriously about the meaning of their worship. I Kings 8 records Solomon's dedication of the Temple. The King reminded the congregation how God had promised David that a temple should be built by his son. Then, according to verse 27, Solomon made the profound statement that God could not be contained within his Temple. He asked God to hear the prayers offered there and ended with the superb plea: 'And when thou hearest, forgive.' The subsequent history of Israel might have been very different if only Solomon had lived up to the level of his own prayer.

The generations went by. It was the prophets, not the kings or the priests, who spoke of new songs. Amos taught one of penitence for social injustice. Hosea sang of God's redeeming love that would not let Israel go despite her unfaithfulness. Isaiah brought a new message of God's holiness which asked for holiness also in his people, a spiritual quality of wholeness manifest in their religious, political and social life.

Then came Jeremiah with a revolutionary teaching of personal responsibility. No longer could men blame the turmoil of their times on the sins of their fathers. Jeremiah insisted on a man's responsibility for his own life. He spoke of a fresh covenant between God and the indiviudal, a new law of God written in the heart.

Jerusalem was overthrown and the people went into exile. Ezekiel had to sing a song very unacceptable both to the exiles and to those left behind in the ruined city. He had to say that they would not be immediately delivered. They must learn to live with their situation and leave the final issue to God.

The last of the songs we might note is that of the unknown prophet who dared to answer the question of innocent suffering. In Isaiah 53, he spoke of a Servant who bears all pain and rejection vicariously for other men. This is the most noble statement of love and service in the Old Testament, to be fulfilled perfectly in Christ himself.

Each of these 'new songs' was a message of faith and spiritual experience. It was an offering to God from a particular situation. But it was also a proclamation to the people directly relevant to their circumstances. The prophetic statement did not foretell the future. It told forth the will of God in the present.

2 The approach to God

How do we approach God in our worship? Sometimes in our prayers we approach him as we would not treat a human father, coming with a long list of requests and little thanksgiving for past blessings. One is reminded of the Victorian schoolboy writing to his parents: 'Gratitude, duty and a view to future advantages, compel me to address you.'

And at times our prayers of penitence have little depth. The King in Hamlet said:

'My words fly up, my thoughts remain below.
Words without thoughts never to heaven go.'

There can be a coldness in the worship of congregations here in the West which contrasts strongly with the enthusiasm of a church in Africa. The sense of the presence of God seems also to be rather more evident in the liturgy of Orthodox churches. Perhaps we need to make more time for silence and for contemplation of God, and for the Spirit to warm our hearts. Then there can be a new depth in our liturgy, a fresh relevance in our prayers to life as it really has to be lived. For worship is giving worth to God and in so doing we give worth to man.

3 Why worship?

The hardest questions are often the simplest ones. If we were asked why we come to church, we might give a variety of answers which would reveal more about ourselves than about the real purpose of worship. Yet the primary purpose should be that of meeting God and that means encounter, open-ness, listening as well as speaking.

Meeting God in worship is not something detached from life. It is from that experience that we can go out expecting to find him in daily living, in people and in situations. We bring the world to God and with him we go out into the world. Isaiah was suddenly aware of God's presence in the Temple. The vision made him acutely conscious of his own unworthiness, but also of the cleansing of his sins. Then he received his vocation to go out as God's agent and minister.

If this is the first object of what we do in church, then it has implications for the kind and quality of worship we offer. For our communion is with God first and only secondarily with each other. Jesus promised that where even two or three were gathered together in his name he would be in the midst of them. 'In his name' is more than a superficial acknowledgement of his presence. It means a living relationship with

Christ and so with each other, and living implies growing. That was why the members of the young church at Ephesus were urged to make new experiments in 'psalms and hymns and spiritual songs', and the Corinthians to sing 'with the spirit and with the understanding also'.

Throughout the New Testament one has a sense of dynamic liturgy related to the growing life of the Church.

4 *Horizontal and vertical*

But worship is not something which we begin afresh when we start a church service. We are only joining in something which is going on throughout the world. In the words of the familiar hymn:

> 'As o'er each continent and island
> The dawn leads on another day,
> The voice of prayer is never silent
> Nor dies the strain of prayer away.'

And it has been going on for centuries here and in eternity. As a sidesman once remarked to a priest: 'Only five here this morning, Vicar. That's not counting the angels!'

This is the song of the Sanctus at the Holy Communion. It flings wide the doors and windows of our limitations to say:

'Therefore with angels and archangels, and with all the company of heaven, we laud and magnify thy glorious name: evermore praising thee, and saying,

Holy, Holy, Holy, Lord God of Hosts, heaven and earth are full of thy glory. Glory be to thee, O Lord most high.'

ADVENT

God's Minority

The symbol of the tourist industry in Israel shows two men carrying between them on their shoulders a long pole from which hangs a bunch of enormous grapes. It is a quirk of history that this modern token of welcome to Israel should be derived from a report about the Promised Land which was rejected by the Israelites, with disastrous consequences to themselves.

The incident is recorded in Numbers 13 and 14. The Israelites had escaped from Egypt. They were encamped in the wilderness of Paran and were undecided as to the next step. Moses decided to send out a scouting party to spy out the land of Canaan. He chose one man from each of the twelve tribes. The commission was away for forty days. On its return, the twelve reported unanimously that the land was exceptionally fruitful. They brought samples of grapes from Eshcol with pomegranates and figs, which must have made the people's mouths water.

Ten of the twelve scouts, however, said that to attempt to enter Canaan would be courting disaster. They said that the inhabitants were of great strength and stature; by comparison, 'we seemed to ourselves like grasshoppers'.

There was a minority report from Caleb and Joshua. They insisted that with God's help nothing was impossible and the Canaanites could be overcome. This advice proved so unpopular that the people tried to stone them. Lamenting that they had ever left Egypt, they demanded a new leader to take them back.

Then the Glory of the Lord appeared at the Tent of Meeting. God was angry with his faithless people. Though Moses pleaded for their forgiveness God insisted that none of the present generation should ever reach the Promised Land. Only Caleb and Joshua should do so. The rest must face forty years of wandering in the wilderness.

1 *The majority was wrong*

The Jewish historian saw this as a turning point in the fortunes of Israel. It explained the fact that although God had called the people out of Egypt, the journey took so long that few of them reach the land of promise. Instead of being the Chosen People they seemed more like the Rejected People.

The account emphasises that this was the people's fault. The

7

twelve scouts had been representative of the whole people. All Israel had been involved in the final choice, in ignoring what God had done for them already and demanding to return to Egypt. Clearly they still had the slave mentality which valued the security of slavery more than the risks and hardship of freedom. It would take years of the wilderness to get Egypt out of their system. When they chose the majority report it was because it accorded with their character at the time.

This was not the end of the majority-minority crisis. Time after time the prophets called Israel to fulfil its calling as the people of God. Only a few responded. Ultimately the prophets came to recognise that the real hope of Israel lay with a faithful Remnant. Its faith would survive the disaster of the Exile to become a foundation for a new Israel as the instrument of God's salvation.

This theme recurs in the New Testament. When Christianity went into action it did so realising that it was only a minority movement—the salt, the leaven in society, 'not many mighty'. Nowhere is there any indication that the early Christians were deeply worried by the prospect of facing the great size of the Roman Empire or the strong opposition of other religions. Yet within three centuries Christianity became, for good or ill, the religion of the Empire.

2 Facing Canaan today

In some ways the mood of Christendom at the present time is similar to that of the Israelites at Paran. There is a nervousness about security and uncomfortable statistics. It seems a far cry from the confidence of a century ago when missionaries could speak of 'the evangelisation of the world within this generation'. Now we are more likely to be emphasising the decline in the membership of the churches themselves. Secularism, Communism, the Permissive Society and the resurgent non-Christian religions, have become like the Sons of Anak 'before whom we seem like grasshoppers'. Yet we are as uneasy about the blind optimists as about the prophets of gloom and doom.

Where lies the truth? When we study the decline in membership of the Church we have to recognise that many of those who belonged to it in the past did so for other than religious reasons. Many diverse factors have produced the present situation. Nevertheless we have to face the possibility that God may be calling the Church to be a minority composed of those who are truly committed to him. Perhaps we are trying too hard to retain the structures, the organisation and the methods which belong to the Church as it was in the past.

We tend to forget that throughout history the greatest changes have been wrought by small groups. Communism began as a minority movement. In one century it has become a world force with as many adherents as has Christianity. Many of the reforms which have brought benefit to mankind, such as the abolition of slavery, have been achieved by the initiative and endeavour of a handful of people. So the problems of the modern world must not be seen as insuperable. They are vulnerable to action by the committed minority.

But committed to what? The answer for the Christian must lie in terms of commitment to truth, the truth about God and about man. This may mean challenging the majority with its structures, false values and wrong methods. Its mythology of power and success and progress has to be questioned. Its policy of treating man as a functional unit and not as the child of God, has to be resisted. The Church must not be afraid to preach an unacceptable Gospel even if this proves as costly as it did at the time for Caleb and Joshua.

3 The minority within

It is pointless to argue that the Church should choose to be an effective minority for God if one is not prepared to do likewise in one's personal life. And witness for truth in the world outside depends on choosing the truth in one's own heart. There is in every one of us a majority which longs for Egypt, and a minority with a vision of Canaan which is prepared to go forward in faith. The two are often in conflict at times of decision, although one may be unaware that this is happening.

What then decides the issue is character. And character is the habit of choice, the consistent attitude of mind, the balance of priorities, the dominant values which make up the self within us. As Archbishop Temple wrote: 'I can be good if I want to. The trouble is that I don't often want to.' Scott Holland put it another way: 'Religion must mean a spiritual life, a converted will, a humble and contrite heart, and a love of God and man.' Those are the criteria we must use when we try to know ourselves, and to discover what are the ruling principles by which we live.

We have to apply an equal realism when we look at our particular problems. Many of them may seem as unconquerable as were the Canaanite Sons of Anak to the ten scouts. This may be true if we were to attempt to deal with them in our own strength. But 'practical Christianity' implies putting faith into practice, above all in the difficult and dark situations that confront us. And faith is not a leap in the dark, but a leap into the light. It means acting not with blind optimism but with intelligent awareness of the power of God in whose mind is the solution to every human problem. As with the Israelites in the wilderness, God offers us a covenant of partnership which is as valid for the new tasks and situations which may lie ahead of us as it has been in the past. We need to have the Christian commonsense to say, with Thomas, 'Lord, I believe. Help thou mine unbelief.'

ADVENT

The rights of man

Twenty six centuries before the Red Cross was founded, an Old Testament prophet preached a revolutionary doctrine that prisoners of war were human beings with rights. This was Amos, a farmer from Judah who went north to Israel. There he began by denouncing the surrounding nations for their cruelty to each other. Damascus had brutally ill-treated Gilead. The cities of the coast sold their captured enemies into slavery. The Ammonites murdered the pregnant women among their captives. Moab desecrated the body of a defeated king.

Amos' audience enjoyed the prophet's condemnation of their neighbours. They may, however, have been surprised to hear that the God of Israel was concerned with the behaviour of other nations towards each other. What was even more startling was the suggestion that victors in war did not have an absolute right to do what they liked with the vanquished. Usually slavery was the best that the defeated could hope for. They had no rights. They had ceased to be regarded as human beings.

1 *Prisoners of war*

Throughout the centuries this attitude persisted, by and large. The treatment of captives depended on the enlightenment of rulers, the force of the demand for revenge or the mollifying influence of people with some religious or social conscience. But still the prisoner as such had no rights.

Then in 1859 a Swiss banker, Jean Henri Dunant, was horrified by the sufferings of the wounded at the Battle of Solferino where the French had defeated the Austrians. He wrote and agitated about this, urging that voluntary agencies should be established to succour the wounded. In 1864 an international conference signed the first Geneva Convention, adopting as its symbol the Red Cross and as its motto *Inter Arma Caritas*— compassion in the midst of battle. This was the beginning of a long hard road which eventually led to the protection of prisoners. Dunant himself suffered years of neglect before his work was ultimately recognised by the award of the first Nobel Peace Prize in 1901. A great victory had been won in the battle for human rights, at least in one realm.

But our own generation is well aware that the struggle goes on. We have seen savage cruelty towards prisoners, the slaughter of millions of Jews, the wholesale destruction of civilian populations, the ferocity of inter-tribal and sectarian conflict, the barbarity of the concentration camp and the sophisticated destruction of the minds of opponents by brain-washing. This has taken place in 'civilised' countries. Are we to conclude that what the pressure of war does is to test something which is fundamental to life in peace as well as in war, a basic concern for the rights of man as a human being?

2 The foundation of rights

This takes us right back to Amos. He turned from denouncing the cruelty of Israel's neighbours to challenge Israel itself about the social injustice within its own life. Though the two themes at first sight may appear to be on very different levels, Amos saw them as manifestations of the same contempt for the rights of man and the same neglect of one's obligations. Because of this, Amos proclaimed, Israel would come to ruin despite its superficial religiosity. Worship was no substitute for justice; neither, he might have added, was charity.

It is a long road from the time of Amos to that of the Declaration of Human Rights made at the United Nations' Assembly in 1948 by 48 nations, with those of the Eastern Bloc and South Africa abstaining. This recognised that 'if man is not to be compelled to have recourse to rebellion against tyranny and oppression, human rights should be protected by rule of law'. That ideal has not always been fulfilled. Even where political freedom and social reform has been achieved after a long struggle, all too often when they come to power the reformers have in their turn suppressed and oppressed those who want to share the new freedom.

What has been at stake is not a political principle but a religious one—the value of man as a person in his own right as the child of God. This is difficult enough for an individual. It requires the self-searching honesty which recognises another human being not as a stereotyped figure, a threat and a competitor, but as someone essentially like oneself. It is even harder for man in the mass in an age when hatred has become part of the climate of opinion. This is the price we pay for insecurity and for our failure to communicate with each other.

Fear, materialism and selfishness make it difficult for men to respect each other's rights. In the family, one or other of these factors leads to the abandonment of the other partner and of children because 'I have a right to live my own life. I have a right to happiness.' In protection of its own interests, a group of people may hold an industry to ransom and cause hardship to thousands. The claim to liberation from censorship may give some the freedom to exploit and corrupt the young. When men live together in any kind of community, small or large, rights and obligations have to be weighed together.

3 What the Bible says

The term 'rights' in its modern connotation is nowhere to be found in the Bible for it does not discuss 'rights' in the abstract. Instead, it speaks about 'right' in terms of uprightness, integrity and justice. This is characteristic of God and he expects it to be characteristic of those who serve him. There are many instances of God's judgement upon those who ignore this obligation, particularly in their treatment of others. Even David sinned in this respect. He was misled by power and perhaps by the example of other Oriental monarchs into thinking that as king he had the right to take another man's wife and arrange for the destruction of her husband. The Commandments too are founded upon basic obligations between man and God and between man and man. In fact the moral codes of the Bible are essentially theological ethics. That is, they derive from the nature of God and the standard which he expects from those who worship him. It would not accept the idea that human conscience can be an infallible guide. It needs education and assistance. The last verse of Judges describes the religious and social disunity of the nation at a time when 'every man did what was right in his own eyes'.

So we come back to God as the source of human rights and to Jesus as manifesting the will of God in his own concern for all men, irrespective of status, success or failure. It may be surprising that neither our Lord nor Paul said anything critical of the social evil of slavery which was so widespread in their time. But what both enunciated was the principle which in the long run was destined to overthrow slavery and many other forms of discrimination. They taught that all men, however unequal may be their abilities or circumstances, are of equal value in the sight of God. When mankind puts this into practice then real progress becomes possible. When it fails to do so, then it lets loose the forces of war, usury and slavery which have destroyed one civilisation after another.

ADVENT

What about that whale?

One of the most valuable and challenging books of the Bible has been largely ignored because of one embarrassing detail in it. This is the book of Jonah. The very idea of a man spending three whole days in the belly of a 'great fish', and surviving, has been too much both for the critics and for the defenders of the Scriptures. Among the latter, some have seized upon our Lord's reference to Jonah's experience as an analogy to his own death and resurrection, as a proof of the historicity of the story. But Jesus was simply making use of a traditional tale well known to his readers. His emphasis lay upon the repentance of the Ninevites as illustrative of the response of the Gentile world. The incident of the great fish is in any case a part of the folk-lore of the Middle East of that time. It is to be found in the traditions of Greece, Egypt and India.

What is remarkable about the book is that it was a work of protest written somewhere between 400 and 200 BC by a highly original thinker. He was appalled by the intensifying nationalism and exclusivism of post-exilic Judaism. He believed that the Almighty was the God of the whole world and not only of the Jews. He was convinced that they had an inescapable vocation to proclaim to other nations the truth about God who would welcome them into fellowship when they repented. So he wrote this dramatic tract. He attributed its authorship to someone from the distant past, the Jonah who was an Israelite prophet mentioned in 2 Kings 14.25. This use of a pseudonym was customary in those days as a means of securing attention for the work by an unknown author. The same thing happened in the first and second centuries AD when there was a flood of apocryphal Gospels, Epistles and Acts, attributed to the Apostles by anonymous authors.

1 *The five act drama*

The story begins with God calling Jonah to go to Nineveh, capital city of the Assyrians, to denounce its wickedness. But Jonah runs away. He takes ship to get away from the country under God's jurisdiction. This is in itself a reminder of the ancient belief that each god's authority was limited to his own country.

There is a storm at sea. The sailors call on their gods for help. Jonah sleeps, unconcerned, down in the hold. The sailors protest at his indifference. The storm continues. The crew decide that this must be because one of them has sinned and their gods are angry. They cast lots to discover the culprit and the lot falls on Jonah. He admits his guilt and tells the sailors to throw him overboard but they are too kind-hearted to do it. They try to row the boat to shore but the storm drives them back. So, pleading with God not to condemn them for their action, they throw Jonah overboard and the storm dies.

Act III consists of Jonah being in the belly of the great fish for three days and nights. During this time he offers a prayer which is a psalm of praise. About its authorship, Martin Luther commented: 'Jonah was not so comfortably placed as to be able to indite so fine a poem!' The poem itself has many quotations from the Psalter.

Act IV shows Jonah cast up on dry land. He goes to Nineveh and proclaims that because of its sinfulness the city is to be destroyed in forty days' time. To his surprise the city repents and the King decrees a fast. God decides that he is not going to punish them.

Act V—the repentance of Nineveh disappoints and angers Jonah. He feels let down by God and has no wish to live. He goes out of the city and sits sulking under the shadow of a tall plant. The next day the plant withers away. Once again, Jonah is so annoyed and miserable that he wants to die. Then God delivers his judgement, but this time it is upon Jonah's attitude. God says that Jonah has been more sorry for the plant than for the 120,000 people of the city who, in their ignorance, 'do not know their right hand from their left', let alone their cattle, for whom God also had a concern.

2 Not me, Lord!

Jonah's reluctance to accept the obligations of being a servant of God is not unique. Many Christians are inclined to think of their membership of the Church as a one-sided contract with God. They prefer the passive to the active, the occasional to the regular, the comfortable to the uncomfortable—like the man who was persuaded to offer a prayer and said: 'use me Lord in whatsoever way thou wilt, but preferably in a purely advisory capacity.'

This can be a real problem when someone has to be appointed to give leadership or a demanding piece of service. To an appeal for help the response can be a deadly silence. It is not much of an excuse to say that one was only waiting to be asked or did not like to appear to be pushing oneself forward. There is no place for false humility when the need is urgent or God is calling the Church to 'buy up the opportunity'. When God calls, God will give the strength.

3 Gloom and Doom

When eventually Jonah preached to Nineveh and the city repented, Jonah was not pleased. At times Christians seem to give way to the same temptation, to prefer being prophets of calamity to being prophets of hope. We have already more than enough proclamation of gloom in the mass media with their apparent preoccupation with sensationalism, cruelty, violence and strife. If this is really 'giving the public what it wants', then we must be suffering from an epidemic of global morbidity. But in fact the television viewer often asks: 'Is there never any good news?'

This is a fair question to put to the Church, too. In an age with so much that is disastrous and so much moral confusion obscuring its very real achievements towards progress, men want to believe in truth and beauty and goodness. Jesus understood this cry from the depths of humanity. As he wept over the coming fate of Jerusalem, he could still bring the good news of the love of God and the evidence of its power at work in human lives. His was, like John the Baptist's a message of repentance but also of hope, the two elements being inextricably linked.

4 The greater realism

Like Jonah, we are under orders to proclaim a call to repentance but also a message of hope. Repentance—yes, for many of our contemporary troubles are fundamentally religious. They arise from the sin of behaving as though one is the centre of the universe, the sin of treating others as though they existed only for one's own benefit and the sin of treating God as though he did not matter. This is not over-simplifying our situation nor does it ignore all the social, economic and other factors in our situation. For in the long run sin or goodness lie in what man does with that situation.

But hope is equally part of the Christian message and it has to be grounded on experience of God and experience of man. There is the evidence of human decency, unselfishness and sacrifice. There is victory over evil. There is the witness of faith and integrity. There is the love which gives and does not count the cost, which reaches beyond death into life.

This is the message which the Christian has to share with the world, not least because he belongs to it. For as John Donne wrote:

'No man is an island, entire of itself; every man is a piece of a continent, a part of the main; if a clod be washed away by the sea, Europe is the less, as well as if a promontory were, as well as if a manor of thy friends or of thine own were. Any

man's death diminishes me, because I am involved in mankind. And therefore never send to know for whom the bell
tolls; it tolls for thee.'

ADVENT

Judgement

'Depend upon it, sir, when a man knows he is to be hanged in
a fortnight, it concentrates the mind wonderfully.'

Dr Samuel Johnson made this remark when he heard of the
repentance of a criminal sentenced to death for forgery. At
that time this was a capital offence. Johnson's comment was
not a sneer. It came from a man who was profoundly concerned about the question of judgement. He had a real anxiety
about punishment for his own sins, tempered by a deep trust
in the forgiveness of Christ as his Saviour. These two themes
are interwoven throughout Johnson's religious life and especially in his prayers. One may wonder how apparent they are
today and if their presence or absence really matters.

1 The Day of the Lord

To some extent the idea which people of any religion have
about judgement reflects their concept of accountability to
their god. In the eighth century BC, the Jews looked forward
to a Day of the Lord with confidence. They saw it as bringing
vengeance against their enemies and restoration of glory to
themselves. They must have felt shocked and insulted when
Amos proclaimed that the Day would bring judgement upon
themselves. They would be punished for such apparently
trifling matters as giving short weight and corrupting judges.
Their elaborate religious ceremonies and regular attendance at
the sanctuaries would not offset their failure to maintain social
justice.

There was even more resentment two centuries later when
Jeremiah refused to promise that a day would soon come when

God would deliver Jerusalem from the Babylonians. Instead, he declared that because of her sins, Judah would have to suffer the purgation of exile.

Centuries passed and once more a day of vengeance was promised in the apocalyptic writings when the Jews were being cruelly oppressed. A similar theme is evident in the Book of Revelation, written to comfort Christians undergoing widespread persecution. There too the enemies are to receive stern judgement, and their innocent victims vindicated.

It is understandable that when people are facing tribulation they should expect the vengeance of God to fall upon their oppressors. What is harder to deal with is in more normal times the idea that divine judgement is never going to affect them because they are essentially in credit with God.

2 Called to account

The ancient prophetic theme returned in the preaching of the Baptist. Many may have expected him to declare the imminence of a day of national vindication. Instead he called for repentance because an entirely different day was at hand. Jesus, too, said nothing about a day of divine vengeance or of the restoration of departed glory to Israel. He foretold the city's destruction and the fulfilment of the vocation of the Chosen People by a New Israel.

In Matthew 25, we have Jesus' description of the Great Assize. Before the Son of Man and his angels, there will be gathered all the nations. He will separate them from one another as a shepherd separates the sheep from the goats. This was familiar territory and his audience may well have been expecting him to prophesy the overthrow of the nation's enemies.

But there was a sudden twist. Blessing and condemnation were to be awarded on a criterion of the fulfilment of the obligations of common humanity between man and man. It took no account of status or race, of ceremonial purity or legal observance. To plead that one was unaware of need or that one had done no deliberate harm to another, was no excuse.

Indifference was as culpable as cruelty. And there was an additional warning. The Son of Man as Judge would so completely identify himself with those whose needs had been met or ignored that what a man did to his fellow he was doing to Christ.

Like Jeremiah of old, Jesus was putting the main emphasis upon personal accountability.

3 Creed and conduct

'He shall come to judge the quick and the dead.' We say these words every time we repeat the creed. What real belief lies behind them? Quite apart from the question of Christ's return for a final judgement, which is hardly ever discussed, it is questionable whether judgement and accountability have any considerable meaning for contemporary Christianity. When belief in any kind of life after death has become so uncertain, the idea of judgement after death has almost disappeared from view.

Yet it was prominent in the teaching of our Lord and it was part of the Gospel which we claim to believe. In that, this life here on earth has value in itself but even more so as preparation for life eternal. What one is and what one does here, seems largely to determine one's state hereafter. So man is accountable to God for what he does with life. And what he suffers here has to be seen in the context of eternity. Because he is a God of justice as well as of love, then to be true to himself, God cannot let evil triumph and virtue fail to bear fruit. For without the hereafter, human life does not ultimately make sense.

Christ's teaching therefore puts this life in a context which gives it meaning and hope. But it also gives it an accountability which we cannot ignore, accountability to God who knows and who cares, who is mercy but who is also justice.

4 Inasmuch . . .

It is sometimes asserted that the very idea of accountability can be harmful, producing a morbid fear of dying, a neurotic preoccupation with petty sins, or the complacent assurance that one's sins will be of no account compared with the sins of those who are destined for an eternal inferno.

But Christ's own teaching justifies none of these charges or concepts. The astonishing feature of the Great Assize is that its sole criterion is that of common humanity. One might even say that in this Jesus is the only perfect Humanist, in the true sense of the word.

Looking back through history, one is compelled to recognise the truth of his words. When common humanity is denied, Christ is being crucified, by wars of religion, by slavery or slums or political corruption, by sweated labour, by terrorism or violence, by commercial exploitation, by racial discrimination or wartime genocide. In the abandoned family, the battered baby, in the progressive polygamy of successions of divorces . . . what is man doing to man today but denying humanity?

We pointed out earlier that when people feel themselves to be in danger or oppression, then they do not think of judgement as applying to themselves. Perhaps the same is happening today because people feel insecure and threatened. Fear makes it hard for them to behave as human beings. Hatred displaces toleration and fellowship. Law then tries force and compulsion but it cannot promote that true accountability which is accepted willingly in the heart and conscience.

The decline of religion has contributed to this situation. It is not so much the loss of belief in judgement after death that matters. What counts is the decline of belief in accountability to God and the refusal to recognise the obligations of being a human being.

That is why one of the most relevant contributions which Christianity can make is to preach the Gospel of belonging— that man and his world belong to God, and that men belong to each other. This is only to put in another way the two Commandments which Jesus said were the ones that gave meaning to all the rest, and to all life: 'Thou shalt love God . . . thou shalt love thy neighbour.' This is the ground of judgement and of hope for humanity.

CHRISTMAS

The Christmas card

Amid the usual display of robins, mistletoe, reindeer and lambs, one Christmas card stood out. It showed a choirboy singing carols on a snowy night outside a house where a merry party was going on. Impatient at receiving no response to his efforts, the boy was pulling at the doorbell and shouting 'O come ON all ye faithful!' He was right. Whatever may be the appeal of Christmas to the outside world, to those who call themselves Christians its challenge is to faith. We can put it this way: when we are at a service in church on Christmas Day, we might ask ourselves just why we are there at all. Is it a matter of habit or belief?

1 *Putting the question*

Imagine that question being put by a television interviewer at Bethlehem. He asks why Mary is there. The answer is one of simple faith. This Jewish girl believed the messenger of God who told her that she was to be the means whereby the Son of God should be born. She accepted the statement that nothing was impossible with God.

Suppose the interviewer asks why Joseph is there. He is the one person whose presence at the Birth is so taken for granted as to be almost left out of the story. St Matthews' Gospel redresses the balance. It sets out the very human dilemma in which Joseph found himself. This honest and kindly man was betrothed to a girl who became pregnant. Unwilling to expose her to scandal, he 'resolved to put her away quietly'. Then according to the first Gospel, the angel of the Lord appeared in a vision. He asked of Joseph an act of deep and unquestioning faith.

The same response was made by the shepherds. They were at work on the night shift. A messenger of God brought them the news of the birth of the Saviour. They went to see for themselves. They saw. They believed.

Finally, the wise men came looking for the birth of a King.

They found only a child born in a stable. But they did not withhold their gifts. 'They fell down and worshipped him.'

This is the Bethlehem story very baldly stated. But each of those present was there because of a response of faith to the call of God. Each found the real meaning of Christmas and enabled God's purpose to be fulfilled.

2 *What does it mean?*

Christmas has a variety of different meanings for different people. For some it is merely 'The Festive Season'. For others it is a time when a family gets together even if during the rest of the year the members of it tend to go their own way. It is for many *par excellence* the children's festival, or it finds us going to church for a rare visit to sing carols. We like to think of it as the season of 'goodwill'. That can mean anything from a rare act of charity to a deep awareness of the needs of the homeless and helpless millions of the world. But even the excesses of commercial exploitation cannot completely obscure the significance of the birth of the Child who was the Christ.

Yet there are many to whom the happier aspects of Christmas are meaningless. There are the folk who by reason of infirmity, old age or isolation have no share in fellowship and family celebration. There are the forgotten ones living in poverty. The message of peace sounds a hollow mockery to people living in the midst of conflict or suffering the ravages of war. Its promise of hope is little comfort to the jobless. Carols of joy have little meaning for the newly bereaved.

If there is a real meaning to Christmas, it must be something which is relevant to the lives of such as these as well as to those who find it easy to celebrate a 'merry' Christmas.

3 *The whole story*

The real point of Christmas lies not in the meaning we are able to attach to it or the way in which we celebrate it. It lies in the meaning which God gave to it. It is his action that counts, not ours. For God 'so loved the world that he gave' his Son to be born into humanity and to give his life for mankind.

Bethlehem is but the beginning, not the sum total, of the Father's action. That is forgotten by those who concentrate exclusively upon the Babe and ignore the Man. Theirs is a sentimental religiosity which refuses to grow up with Jesus. They delight in the stable because it appears to demand nothing from them, although as we have already seen, it asks for a searching response of faith. That faith accepts the fact that the consequence of the birth was the death and resurrection. As Paul recognised, Christ's self-emptying of glory to become Incarnate was the beginning, and the ending was the humbling of the Cross. The love was the same throughout. So was the triumph of light over darkness, of good over evil, of life over death. The meaning of Christmas, therefore, is not to be confined to the stable. It relates to the whole of Christ's life, and ours.

4 Method and mystery

The Incarnation and the Atonement are the two fundamental doctrines of Christendom. They are doctrines embodied in the experience of the disciples as they 'companied with' Jesus during his lifetime, as they reflected later on that experience and were subsequently led by the Spirit 'into all truth'. It is difficult for us to appreciate how revolutionary a leap of faith this demanded of men brought up as Jews and unprepared for this exposure to an entirely new set of facts. But the ground of their faith was their readiness to believe in God as willing to act in the human situation. This was the crucial 'miracle' which they were prepared to accept, in the record of Bethlehem and of Jerusalem thirty years later. Their understanding and explanation of it grew through the years. By the time of the Gospels according to St Luke and St Matthew the doctrine of the Virgin Birth had been formulated as the 'mode' of the Incarnation. This is in itself surprising, for Jews rejected the Hellenistic stories about children of divine birth born to women as a result of liaisons with gods. Moreover there was nothing in Jewish tradition which prophesied a virgin birth. In the only possibly relevant passage, in Isaiah 7.14, the prophet used the word *almah*. This simply meant a young woman and the writer was looking to a time in the immediate future when deliverance would come through a new leader. The fact that the Virgin Birth was not mentioned in the earliest records of the New Testament proves nothing. At that time Christians were looking forward to Christ's imminent return, not analysing the past. They were concerned with Christ's Divine Sonship and this is not dependent upon the physical mode of his conception or birth. Nor does his assumption of human nature depend upon whether Jesus had one, or two, human parents.

We are faced here with the joyful mystery of Christmas. And the mystery lies not in *how* it happened but in *why* it happened. In the last generation or two men have reacted against the idea of mystery. They have been prepared to accept only what they could 'prove' and explain in material terms, in respect of the universe and man within it. Their idea of God has been scaled down to fit their pragmatism. They have turned Christ from Saviour into Idealist. Now we are beginning to see that all this has somehow gone wrong. Man is still a mystery and so is his universe. Men are searching anew after the transcendence and the immanence of God. They are looking for light and truth more absolute than the truths which men proclaim to themselves. They are seeking a ground of hope more certain than the successive false hopes of history. Perhaps like the Prodigal Son, man is 'coming to himself' and coming home to the Father whose infinite love is the greatest mystery of all.

EPIPHANY

The two-faced god

Time has always been a mystery to man. From the earliest days its periods, its beginnings and endings, were vested with religious significance. The start of a new year was of particular importance. It was thought by the Romans to be under the protection of one of the earliest of their gods, Janus, who has given his name to our first month. He was believed to preside over the start of any new enterprise for his was 'the spirit of opening'. He was regarded with such respect that only the king could be his high priest. Janus was represented in sculpture as having two faces, one looking backward and one looking forward. His commemoration came soon after the winter solstice when men were looking hopefully towards the spring.

In the Christian era, however, March came to be thought of as the first month of the year. Then there was a change from the Julian to the Gregorian calendar. In Britain this took place in 1752 and once again January was the beginning of the year.

1 *The continuity of life*

The ways in which man divided time reflected his view about life itself. The first patterns were based on the cycles of nature. For the early nomad Semites to whom the Jews belong, the most significant rhythm was that of the moon. The Hebrew word for a year was *shanah* and that literally meant 'change', relating to the sequence of the seasons and the agricultural work consequent upon them. But the Jews thought of time as a continuous stream in which past, present and future flowed into each other. So a man's identity was based upon his line of ancestry. The attention given to the genealogies of Jesus in Matthew 1 and Luke 3 would not have been regarded as exceptional. Then the orthodox theory about survival beyond death allowed man to believe that he had some continuity in his children. The link between past and present was expressed also in the idea that contemporary troubles were the fruit of the sins of the past.

The people also had a strong sense of historical and corporate continuity as a tribe, and later as a nation. They attached great importance to their roots in the land itself (although, perhaps surprisingly, this theme is totally absent from the teaching of Jesus). An example of this is to be found in Naboth's refusal to part with his vineyard to King Ahab. This deep attachment to territory remains to this day an important factor in Middle East politics.

The psalmists and prophets emphasised a different continuity, that of the convenant relationship with God. He had kept his promise to save Israel in the past and would do so in the future. On the other hand, they had the responsibility of fulfilling their part of the compact and this obligation was handed down from generation to generation. The passage of time made no difference to it.

2 Time and the Gospel

To the Old Testament concept of time, the New Testament brought a new dimension and a new urgency. This is evident in the way in which the Gospel story opens with the proclamation of the Baptist that the crisis has come. While there is time, men must repent. Then from the obscurity of Nazareth, Jesus suddenly begins his mission and it was all over in two years. Mark presents it as a rapid sequence of events—he used the word 'straightway' twice as many times as do the other three evangelists together.

Throughout the teaching of Jesus there is a note of urgency. Men are frequently told to watch and pray for they know not the hour when they will be called to account. The Kingdom is upon them. The New Age is being inaugurated.

The Church became the community of the new age. For a period its time-scale was short. This influenced its attitude to communal organisation, to evangelism, to money and even to marriage. But the Lord did not return, at least not in the way in which this had been expected. So the time-scale had to change. The Christians had to get used to the idea of indefinite postponement, stretching perhaps beyond their present generation. The process of readjustment could be difficult. But they coped with it remarkably effectively. They made records of what Jesus had said and done, to pass on to future generations. They worked out ways of ministry and service. They accepted the possibility that they themselves might die before their Lord's return. And they had the impertinence to look upon the pomp and glory of the empire as but a passing vanity.

Some of them saw history itself as in the hand of God. This was one of the inspired contributions of Paul. In Galatians 4.4, he wrote: 'When the time had fully come, God sent forth his son, born of a woman, born under the law, to redeem those who were under the law, so that we might receive adoption as sons.' For decades, scholars have argued over Paul's idea that the time was ripe, as to whether, for instance, he meant that the readiness lay in the desperate condition of the world or in the mysterious purpose of God.

The last book in the New Testament is very much concerned with time, written as it was to strengthen a Church weakened by ruthless persecution and desperately worried about the massacres of the innocent. It tried to keep the balance between present trials and the future vindication of the godly. Not all Christian sects have kept this balance. They have succumbed to the temptation to misinterpret the signs of the times and take them to indicate that the End has come. But this is the mistake against which Christ gave an express warning in Matthew 24.

3 The time is now

The biblical ideas about time seem to have given the people of those days a kind of security and an ability to accept the vicissitudes of life with patience. These appear to be lacking in the present age when we become obsessed with its problems. We are nostalgic for departed glories and glamorise the past as the good old days, or else we are impatient for the imagined paradise of the future. But the New Testament puts high value on the 'Now' of the present tense as the moment of opportunity, to be seen in the context of eternity.

If one looks back in retrospect, it should be in order that one may better understand what is happening in the present. This is quite different from the backward look which leads not to penitence but to regret. Many a recollection provokes us to lament . . . 'If only . . . ' and to cherish the illusion that if we had acted differently or if we had had better luck, then we should be happier people today. We do this particularly if we are the kind of people who think that happiness is something which comes to us from outside. But in fact it happens from within, from our reaction to others or to events. And that reaction tends to be consistent. Personality can be its own prison, and age does not alter this. It is not what time does to us that matters so much as what we do with time.

4 *Time for God*

We realise that the time we give to people can affect our relationships with them, especially with those we say we love. The same is true of our relation to God, in respect of the amount of time we give to worship and to prayer, not least in bringing God into the making of decisions. And we should be doing this because we know that all our time is really his; our life itself is something in which we exercise a stewardship to God. This is the basis of our Christian commitment. Yet that is one of the most thorny problems of Christianity today. Our forefathers tended to have a deeper sense of commitment in this respect. They saw vocation to the ordained ministry, to missionary service or to the religious orders, in terms of lifetime allegiance. They took the same view of baptism and confirmation and marriage. Nowadays we are inclined to apply to all these the 'short-term contract' standard of the secular world and to believe that somehow lifelong commitment is too much to ask of human nature. Yet the ground of commitment lies not in our own resources but in the grace of God enabling us to fulfil it. So our prayer must be for a renewal of the faith which puts our time and the whole of our life into the hand of God with joyous confidence.

EPIPHANY

He was made manifest

'Christmas comes but once a year' and it is very soon over. Yet the restriction of its celebration to a day or two, is a comparatively recent development. Even a century ago the Twelve Days were being kept with appropriate festivities. Now, perhaps under the pressure of commercialism, we tend to anticipate the Feast of the Nativity. But Christian tradition in the past saw this Day as leading to a season celebrating the continuing revelation of God in Christ.

It began with the Epiphany, the manifestation to the wise men who came and saw and worshipped. Their gifts of gold, frankincense and myrrh are still commemorated in the gifts which the Sovereign offers at a service on this day in the Chapel Royal in London.

The Prayer Book Gospels for the next four Sundays continue the story. First, Christ reveals himself in the Temple when a boy of twelve. His insight amazes the scholars. His parents are mystified by his reply to their gentle rebuke: 'Did you not know that I must be in my Father's House?'

Next comes what John calls 'the beginning of signs'. This is the miracle at Cana when Jesus stepped in at a domestic crisis and secretly revealed his power over material things.

Then we have an account of his power of healing, when he cured a leper and the centurion's servant. The circumstances foreshadow the way in which Christ's power will range beyond barriers of race and nation.

On the fourth Sunday, the Gospel sets Epiphany in the context of the cure of a man 'possessed with devils'. Here is Christ engaged in the conflict between the powers of good and the forces of evil.

1 *The revelation continues*

This arrangement of narratives may seem somewhat artificial. But it only reflects the belief of the first Christians that in Christ God was continuing the revelation of himself which was evident throughout his dealings with Israel. This was a crucial point of division between the Christians and Jews, the latter holding to the Law and the Prophets as in the main the totality of revelation. The Christians laid great store by the links between the ways in which God had shown himself in the past and the fresh revelation in Christ. He was the fulfilment of God's promise.

They believed that the revelation would continue. They took seriously Christ's promise that his Spirit would guide him into truth. The remarkable response of Gentiles to their preaching and Paul's interpretation of the 'mystery' of the Gospel, led them to realise eventually that the mission to the Gentile world was what God was showing them to be his will.

They believed that the Spirit was leading them into new ways which demanded new responses. One of these was the collection of what one might call foundation documents. At first the Church had no 'Bible' of its own other than the Old Testament. Gradually it came to collect the letters of the Apostles and then the Gospels. In the second century many apocryphal Gospels, Epistles and apostolic Acts came to be circulated. The Church patiently worked its way through these to establish a Canon of Scriptures which could be accepted as valid and in true accord with the life of Jesus and with their experience of his continuing self-revelation. Facing the challenges of heresy, it began to define its faith in credal form.

It is however understandable that in a hostile world the Church should have found it difficult to appreciate that God's revelation could be going on outside itself. This attitude was summed up in Augustine's dictum: 'No salvation exists outside the Church.' It was centuries before the Renaissance opened men's eyes to the richness and wisdom of the ancient world, to a new understanding of humanity and a new evaluation of science. In more recent generations there has been much controversy over developments in many branches of science which have appeared to challenge the Church's concept of God, particularly in respect of revelation.

2 *What God reveals*

We have come to see perhaps as one result of such controversies, that God's self-revelation is not a closed book and that it continues inside and outside the Church. But this idea presents its own problems, not least for the inner life of the

Church. He may be calling it to make radical changes in its whole way of life, so that it might be a more effective instrument for his purpose. In the movement towards unity, for example, we have to examine critically even the basic principles which we take for granted. We assume that unity as we envisage it is necessarily what God wants. We may regard as indispensable certain traditions which each Church brings to the ecumenical development. Yet in fact it is hard for us to distinguish between principles and prejudices, or to recognise that what any denomination regards as its greatest strength may be its greatest weakness. In this, as in any part of Christian endeavour, there is always a risk that men will attribute to divine revelation what are essentially their own man-made ideas and plans.

3 Revelation and response

The theme that runs through the Epiphany gives the guide to the understanding of revelation. In each instance quoted above, Jesus was manifesting himself in response to a human need, whether conscious or otherwise. The Magi looking for a Kingdom, the Temple needing renewal from one who was the Child of God, the family in need of practical help, the leper and the centurion's boy wanting health—these were real persons standing for all humanity. And God continues to reveal himself in human situations, which ask for a response from a sensitive Church.

He also shows himself in the movements of mankind. Man has been discovering much about his universe, in arts and sciences and technology, in sociology and psychology. Many of those involved in these realms are just as concerned as Christians are about human values and relationships, about the nature of truth and the purpose of life. If we really believe that this is God's universe and that he is the source of all truth, then we must be prepared to learn from that truth when it is discovered by others. Christians have done this already to some extent, for example, in accepting psychology's help towards the deeper understanding of the mainsprings of human personality.

Science is not infallible. Often the greater the scientist, the greater is his reluctance to claim absolute knowledge. But science should be widening our awareness of the infinity of the power of God—that is, unless our 'image of God' is too small to allow us to expand our horizons.

If our contemporary situation encourages us to look for God revealing himself in new ways of this kind, it also calls us to fresh understanding of humanity itself. If Christianity offers a way of redemption, salvation and reconciliation as the heart of its Gospel, then those terms have to be 'earthed' in realistic application. Of course man has to be redeemed and liberated from slavery to sin within himself, or from the prison of a world which treats him as a thing—just like the slave of the first century. But this has to go along with the redeeming of society. Of course man needs salvation. For this means wholeness and integrity in the individual and in the community. Of course he needs reconciliation, to himself as well as to other men and to God. The terms used may be those of everyday life as Paul knew it. The truths behind them are relevant to everyday life as we know it. For this is the Gospel of Jesus Christ who is 'the same yesterday and today and for ever'.

EPIPHANY

Senior citizens

At first sight, the Presentation in the Temple is just one more of Luke's delightful 'human interest' stories about the childhood of Jesus. A husband and wife came up from the country with the babe, carrying the traditional offering of 'a pair of doves or two young pigeons'. The offering was made and a blessing given. All over in a few minutes, it was hardly noticed by the crowds thronging the Temple.

But among them was an old man named Simeon. He was watching for 'the consolation of Israel' and was convinced that he would not die before he had seen the Messiah. Possibly he was treated indulgently as an old fellow with a harmless obsession. But when the child was brought in, Simeon knew that this was what he had been waiting for. He took the baby up in his arms, and gave thanks to God in the superb words of the *Nunc Dimittis*. But he warned that the child would bring conflict and heart-searching, not least to his mother. Then, Luke adds, an aged prophetess Anna also welcomed the child as Messiah. She spoke of him 'to all who were looking for the redemption of Jerusalem'. And Mary and Joseph went home to Nazareth.

In the midst of the turmoil of Palestine, its political unrest and religious divisions, these two old people had gone on believing and hoping and praying. When their prayers were answered, they responded to the unexpected, with faith and hope and love.

1 *Age has its problems*

In the time of Jesus the aged were venerated as the guardians of tradition and repositories of wisdom and experience. They played their part in the transmission of culture from one generation to the next. They had an important role in the life of the community, not least in respect of the religious education of the young.

Times have changed and with them the status of the elderly. One reason for this has been the denigration of past experience as largely irrelevant to the contemporary situation. Another is the gradual disappearance in western society of the 'extended family' and with it the role of the aged as members of that family. 'Honour thy father and thy mother' becomes a responsibility to be transferred to the State. The aged dislike being thought of as receivers of assistance instead of as contributors to the welfare of everyone. It is hard for them to find meaning in a society which appears to have no use for them. The widespread effect of all this on morale is a problem of growing importance, not least because, owing to the rapid decline in the birth-rate, the numbers of the retired assume an increasing proportion of the whole population.

The reaction of the elderly to this changed situation varies widely. It cannot be assumed that old age is in every case a 'problem', any more than is middle age or youth. Simeon and Anna are typical of those to whom age made little difference in respect of their being truly young in hope and young in heart. They showed no signs of the nostalgia which is a hazard of growing old. It is easy to pine for the 'good old days', without remembering that for some they may have been the bad old days. It is equally easy to blame the present generations for current ills, without recognising that many of these troubles were caused by the apathy and errors of the last generation. The Jewish idea of social continuity, expressed in the saying that 'the fathers have eaten sour grapes and the children's teeth are set on edge', has much evidence to support it. As we grow old, we may glamorise the past. We may also be equally unrealistic about ourselves. We do not necessarily become easier to live with, more wise or even better Christians. We can grow more demanding, more addicted to self-pity and even—to put it bluntly—more boring than we were in the past. The fact is that in the modern world at any state of life we receive the respect we deserve because of what we are in ourselves, not because of any accident of age.

2 *The gifts of age*

What age should bring us is a new dimension of time—time to think and pray, time to give others the three gifts of faith and hope and love which Simeon and Anna offered to such good effect. On the gift of faith, it is evident that nowadays it is the grandparents, more than parents, who are concerned to bring the children for baptism. And one is well aware of their contribution in worship, in prayer groups, in visiting the sick and the newcomer, and not least in private prayer. A man who was to undergo a serious operation had a letter from an aged and bedridden friend. She wrote from experience of a similar operation and of a long and tedious recuperation. She said that she knew all too well how grim could be the long sleepless hours of the night. She said that she was going to set her alarm clock for 3 a.m. At that time she would pray for her friend for a quarter of an hour every night. So he could know that he would not be alone . . .

Her gift of prayer was a valuable use of something of which we have too much in old age—and that is time. It can hang heavily on our hands with so little happening to bring us interest and expectation. Yet it can be fruitful if we look on it as a commodity which we have to share with others. For instance, if the 'extended family' is less evident than it was formerly, the support which the older members used to give to the younger ones in it, can sometimes be offered by the older neighbours. They can become the substitute aunts and uncles for the home where the children's parents are both working. The elderly friends may have time to be good listeners to the adolescent and so to bridge a generation gap. They have time also to make contact with the new neighbour in the anonymous sprawl of urban life. These are not superficial or sentimental suggestions for ways in which the elderly may occupy their time. The fact is that very considerable problems of personality and relationships are developing in our urban society. These cannot begin to be solved except by person-to-person contact and service from people who care about their fellow men and who have time to spare for them. In this realm the contribution which the 'senior citizen' can make, may be of even greater importance than it has been in the past.

The Christian's response to this situation must start from his recognition that no one retires from being a Christian any more than he retires from being a human being. And vocation is not a call from God which can operate only when one is young. John Wesley prayed: 'Lord, let me not live to be useless.' He was not thinking with dread of a decrepit old age but seeing that one's usefulness to God was the measure of faith and happiness at any age. Towards the end of his life the Apostle Paul went on fulfilling his vocation despite his prison of circumstances. Because he had done so, he could know he had finished his course—and 'kept the faith'. And that is the important point. For however young or old we may be, if we keep faith in God and keep faith with God, then like Simeon and Anna we are ready to respond with gladness to the call of God.

EPIPHANY

Paul on TV

To bridge the gap of nineteen centuries between the world Christ knew and the world today, we need to use our imaginations. That does not just mean trying to think what life was like then. It should mean also thinking of our way of life from the angle of the first century. How would early Christianity have appeared to the mass-media of radio and television? Imagine an interview with Saint Paul, for example . . .

1 *Direct from Rome*

Interviewer   Tonight we bring you the latest in our series of interviews with prominent personalities on the question 'What difference has your philosophy made to your life?' It comes from our Outside Broadcast studio under the Coliseum. Our guest is that well-known Christian evangelist Paul of Tarsus.

    I understand, Paul, that you were brought up as a Jew. Why did you become a Christian?

Paul   The simple answer is that I had to. It's true that I was a Jew and a very definite and loyal one. So loyal that I spent an immense amount of time and effort attacking the Christians. I considered them to be dangerous enemies of the true religion. I had them driven from their homes and imprisoned. In fact I was largely responsible for the breakup of the Christian Church in Jerusalem. Then I saw one of them being stoned to death for his faith, a young man named Stephen. He died nobly, forgiving his destroyers. That disturbed me. It haunted me. My reaction was to become even more hostile to Christianity.

Then suddenly in a vision on the road to Damascus, I met the founder of Christianity, Jesus of Nazareth. He challenged me and I became a Christian.

Interviewer   I suppose that your conversion was a great capture for the Church. Were you welcomed with open arms?

Paul   No. Far from it. They thought I was a spy. It was years before they trusted me and I owe that as much as anything to a man called Barnabas, a great saint who was prepared to give me the blessed gift of the benefit of the doubt.

Interviewer   So then they accepted you as a leader?

Paul   Not for a long time. I remained an ordinary member of the Church, earning my living as a tentmaker and trying to win over my fellow Jews. Then it gradually came over me that this was not my real job. I felt that God was calling me to take the good news of the Gospel to the outside world. I believed that you Gentiles were just as much the children of God as were the Jews. That led me to the revolutionary conclusion that the Gentiles could become Christian by making the act of faith without necessarily conforming to the Law which the Jews obeyed.

Interviewer   Well, that's what one might call a theological point and perhaps we might discuss it some time on another programme. But to get back to your own career—were you successful in your work?

Paul   It depends on what you mean by success. If you measure it in terms of popularity, then the answer is 'No'. It turned out all too often to be a life of rejection. I was publicly flogged, often homeless, chased out of cities, regarded with suspicion by some of my fellow Christians and eventually denounced by my fellow Jews who tried to assassinate me.

Interviewer   So what have you to show for it all?

Paul Let's see ... a dozen or so little churches around the Mediterranean consisting mainly of small groups of people, many of them slaves—meeting secretly in houses, usually. Some strong, some weak. Some growing. Some dying out. But they have a great faith in Jesus Christ as their Risen Lord. They worship together. They help each other ... I think they'll survive, perhaps even longer than the Empire.

Interviewer My dear sir, you can't be serious! But I admire your confidence anyway. Now to come back to yourself, for a moment. I understand that you were a young man with a brilliant future. You might well have become a religious lawyer of international reputation. And of course you might have married and had a family as I understand all good Jews are expected to do. You seem to have given up so much. What are your prospects now?

Paul As far as this world is concerned, I haven't any. I have just been informed that tomorrow I am to die, by decree of the Emperor. But death is not all that important. I have finished my course. I have done what I was called to do years ago on that Damascus road, by my Risen Lord. It was that event which made all the difference to my life—and it makes all the difference to my life after death.

Interviewer Well that concludes our interview. Thank you, Paul, thank you very much indeed ... In our interview next week ....

2 *A question of difference*

In our imaginary interview we posed the question: 'What difference has it made to your life to be a Christian?' We rarely ask that particular question. Instead, if we bother about difference at all it is in terms of comparison with other people. We ask how Christians compare with their fellowmen in kindness, goodness, service, integrity, unselfishness and so on. This is a very worthwhile exercise and the results are not always comfortable and comforting, if we make an honest inquiry.

It is an important inquiry also because the world genuinely wants to know what difference it makes to be a Christian. It wants to see that distinctiveness demonstrated.

Our interview poses a question at a deeper level. It does not compare a Christian with a non-Christian. It asks him to compare himself as he is, with himself as he might have been, if he had not been a Christian, or with himself as he is now with what he was like a year or more ago. What have we learned from life and learned about ourselves? But learning implies growth in the spiritual life, in our prayers, in our worship, in our capacity to face suffering and in our readiness to give service to God and man. That growth takes place when we are willing to let the fact of our being Christians, the fact of our faith, make a difference to our decisions and to our relationships. Then the difference that is effective within us becomes evident in our whole manner of life—as it did with Saint Paul.

EPIPHANY

The embarrassed saint?

Some of our popular customs have a strange mixture of origins. The popular practice of sending Valentine cards on 14 February owes nothing to the third-century saint. It comes from a belief, mentioned by Chaucer in the fourteenth century, that on this day the birds begin to choose their mates. That is what really lies behind the fact that millions of Valentines are sent every year, as tokens of love or for a joke. They may even be distributed by commercial firms wooing customers in a business courtship!

This is a far cry from the memory of the saint who according to tradition was martyred on this day in AD 270 because of his faith and his love. He had been gaoled for having helped some prisoners who were under sentence of death. In prison he healed the gaoler's daughter and converted the whole family to Christianity. He did this by his teaching and, even more, by his infectious example. The Roman authorities thought such a man too dangerous to live. So they had him beaten with clubs and then beheaded. Just one martyr among thousands. Valentine might have been forgotten but for this strange association of the date of his martyrdom with a day which already figured prominently in popular superstition. The Church has never been comfortable about the connection and it is significant that no churches have ever been dedicated in his honour.

It is curious that in this age which claims to be sophisticated and unsentimental, the custom of sending Valentines should have remained so popular. Astute commercial propaganda cannot be the only reason for this. It may be that we are sentimentalists at heart even if we do not admit it, or that we are trying to prove that we mean something to somebody. At least the Valentine can be an indication that the sender is not taking the recipient for granted. It may even be a token of love.

1 Tokens of love

To keep love alive and growing takes more than attitudes of mind. Love has to be expressed in deed as well as in word. The warmth of courtship dies away under the chill weight of a 'take-it-for-granted' attitude in a marriage, where neither partner bothers to show the other appreciation. The marriage vows include the promise to cherish and fulfilling this gives warmth to the other obligations.

As the child grows up within the family, an important part of his nurturing is the training in giving as well as in receiving. We have tended to forget this in recent years when we have overemphasised 'child-centredness' in education as in family life. It is also overshadowed by the welfare-state outlook which is inclined to make us all too concerned about getting our share of what the State can provide. Even in the local community there has been a marked change as regards 'charity'. In many towns and villages there are survivals of ancient charitable foundations established by benefactors of past generations. They sought to make provision for the poor, the education and apprenticing of the young or the care of the aged. Now we look to the State to make this provision. While it is true that charity in the old sense must never be a substitute for social justice, yet we are losing something when we ·transfer all responsibility to the State. It can make the contributor irresponsible and give the recipient a feeling of being depersonalised, and inclined to think that no one really cares about him as a human being. That is why there is such value in the person-to-person voluntary service which is so encouraging in modern community life, given by young people looking after the elderly, by voluntary organisations caring for the lonely infirm and by 'good neighbour' campaigns. This is the caring community overcoming the deadening effect of living in a mass society. It is true charity because it is loving directly involved in responsible action.

2 *The ultimate token*

Saint Valentine gave his life as the token of his love. It is for this he deserves to be remembered. By so doing, he was following the example of his Master Jesus Christ who was himself the token of the love of God. That love is so easily taken for granted, as if the attitude of the Father were only a vague benevolence which asked no questions. The prophets like Amos and Hosea saw it differently. They believed that God cared deeply about his people, loving Israel despite her betrayal of him, yet having to correct her for her own sake. As Jeremiah realised, there comes a time when the very love of God requires him to let his people endure suffering so that they may be redeemed.

The ultimate proof of God's love, as Saint John put it, was that 'He gave his only-begotten Son, that whosoever believeth in him should not perish but have everlasting life. For God sent not his Son into the world to condemn the world, but that the world through him should be saved.' This amazing statement describes God as thinking the world worth saving,

42

despite all its faults and betrayal of him. Jesus himself said that he came not to call the righteous but sinners. This is one of the great truths of salvation, that the gift of love does not depend on the merit of the recipient. It asks only for the response of faith and of love.

3 Love in action

It was this response of faith and love that Paul described in detail to the Corinthians. He was writing to a church which was torn by division, confused in its thinking about morals and rent by claims of status. So he did not write about love in general terms but analysed its implications. In 1 Corinthians 13, he did this in directly practical terms.

He said that preaching, prophesy, religious conviction, acts of charity and even martyrdom are useless without love. Then he turned to the positive side of it. Love is patient and kind. Free from boasting and jealousy, it does not demand its own way. It is not easily irritated or resentful. It takes no pleasure in evil. Love is willing to accept suffering. It has a profound faith, a constant hope and a lasting endurance. This is the high ideal which was realised only in Christ. If one substitutes the name of Jesus for 'love' throughout this chapter, the origin of Paul's vision becomes evident.

Paul certainly never intended this famous chapter to be treated as superb literature, as if that were the end of the matter. It is in fact like a questionnaire to be applied in detail to the daily life of the Corinthian in the first century or the Christian in the twentieth.

Love is patient—towards those whom we do not understand as well as those we love. It is kind—to the stupid and the undeserving as well as to those who are kind to us. It simply leaves no room for boasting or jealousy or self-assertion. Nor is it quick to take offence or to feel ill-treated. Love takes no pleasure in evil and it does not feel a morbid interest in the sins of the world. In true humility it is prepared to admit when it is in the wrong—in Oliver Cromwell's words: 'I beseech you in the bowels of Christ to think that ye may be mistaken.'

Item by item Paul brings us away from high-minded senti-mentalising about love, to the practical tests of love in thought and word and deed every day of our lives. And from his own experience he adds a final thought: that love is the token of maturity of soul and mind. For growing in grace means growing in love.

This analysis of love in action is not a cold-blooded exercise. It is necessary in any age like our own which escapes from the responsibility of loving by generalising it. When Saint Augustine wrote: 'Love and do what you like,' the point of his emphasis was on the quality of love not on 'do what you like'. The permissive society reverses the emphasis. Self-fulfilment is the measure of behaviour and love becomes the after-thought. So it becomes transitory and superficial, giving pleasure but not happiness. It is when the loving becomes the reflection of the love of God and involves the whole man in a whole relationship, that the 'do what you like' takes on a new meaning. The Doing comes within the scope of the Loving and it shows itself by the tokens of joy and consideration, or warm affection and ready service. And those tokens are given not on one day in the year but readily throughout the whole of life.

EPIPHANY

Jesus . . . out!

Most of us have to face a certain amount of criticism during our lifetime. Normally it does not worry us much. If it is constructive and we are sensible about it, then it can do us good. If it is merely destructive and baseless, then we can ignore it, taking refuge perhaps in the thought that our critics are mistaken.

Fortunately it rarely happens that we feel we are being positively hated, as individuals or as belonging to a nation. One of the disturbing aspects of foreign travel is that we can sometimes find ourselves in a country which takes a poor view of us as British. We may find ourselves regarded with hostility simply because of the colour of our skins. Then the irrationality of antagonism and hatred hits us acutely. Yet this was an experience from which Jesus suffered, unbelievable as this may seem.

1 *Pigs or people?*

It happened to him once when he was on the east side of the lake of Galilee, not far from what are called today the Golan Heights. He encountered the bizarre figure of a madman, naked and unkempt, living among the tombs well away from the outskirts of town. The three synoptic gospels record the meeting and the restoration of the demoniac to sanity. So far, so good; this was one more instance of the compassion of Jesus and his power over unclean spirits.

What followed was not so good. Possibly because they had been disturbed by the cries of the sufferer, a herd of pigs ran madly down the slope and over the precipice to drown in the lake. The herdsmen saw what had occurred. They raced back to the town and reported what had happened to the pigs, and to the demoniac. Then, as Luke 8.35 reports, the townsfolk came out in a body to meet Jesus and 'when they saw him they begged him to leave their neighbourhood'.

They might have had many sick people in need of healing. They might have heard Jesus' teaching, with benefit to themselves. But instead they told him to get out of their country. Jesus had advised his disciples not to waste their time in any village or district which rejected them. So, without protest, he went back to the boat and they all crossed over to the other side. The Gadarenes had put pigs before people, and profit before truth.

This was not the only occasion when the barrier of self-interest prevented a response to Jesus. At the top level of power, the Jewish leaders saw him as a threat to their status. Pilate knew he was condemning an innocent man. He was terrified of giving the Jews ground for one more official complaint about him to Rome. Even among those who came near to accepting him, there were last-minute obstacles. For one, it was the excuse of family ties. Another could not face the loss of the very wealth which was failing to give him happiness. Even some of Christ's secret followers like Nicodemus and Joseph of Arimathea were afraid to come out into the open. And of course the ultimate tragedy was that of Judas. We shall never know what were the real motives for the betrayal of his Master by this odd-man-out among the disciples, the only Southerner in a group of Northerners. It may have been simply the despairing desire to get some profit for himself out of what he thought to be a hopeless situation.

2 *People matter*

Ever since the story of Cain and Abel, mankind has suffered from the tendency to put self-interest above common humanity and the acceptance of truth. Slavery and oppression, war and conquest have marched over human lives as if they were of no consequence. Religions have at times been as ruthless as ideologies in driving towards their objectives at the cost of humanity. They have claimed to be doing this as a matter of principle when it may have been a matter of prejudice, fear or lust for power.

The priority of people as human beings is just as difficult to maintain in contemporary society. Progress and efficiency are believed to be dependent on size. So people are put in ever larger groups for housing, employment, education, welfare and administrative purposes. But this process of collectivisation tends to be destructive of real efficiency and progress, because it seems to be dehumanising. Man begins to feel that he is being regarded as a depersonalised object of manipulation. He is unable to find meaning, and to establish relationships, in a group too large for his comprehension. His reaction may range from apathy to suspicion, from frustration to violence. He will not accept responsibility when he believes that the state treats him as irresponsible and less than human. In Gadarene terms, he is a pig not a person.

There is evidence of a strong reaction against this process, which was believed to be the panacea for almost all human troubles, in the 1950s and 1960s. But a nostalgia for the 'good old days' of the village community and the small unit is not enough. A new direction in planning, in the best sense of the word, is needed from people who are concerned to give the right place to human values in developing man's society. To do this Christianity must be willing to play its part, not as a critical spectator, but as a participant committed to the Kingdom of God as an ideal realisable here in God's world.

3 *Person to Person*

What we believe to be necessary on the large scale has also to be made effective on the small scale of personal contact. Jesus gave his priority to the healing of one broken and outcast man, and his restoration to life and sanity. He did not ignore the individual situation while laying down rules on the general issues. In fact it is often true that person-to-person action is the most effective contribution to the wider solution. Moreover, sometimes it can initiate a movement in which many others are involved. But it has value in itself, wherever it happens.

Here is a teacher spending himself to assist the backward child to catch up with the rest of the class. A social worker helps the misfit to take his place in the community, or brings the wayward girl back to the family which has to be helped to receive her. In a factory one of the older hands takes the trouble to assist the young apprentice to settle in to his work in the factory. A 'senior citizen' in a youth club is there to provide an understanding ear for the youngster whose parents are too busy to listen to him. A student is led to choose a career where the prospect of giving service is greater than that of receiving high rewards.

The above are all instances taken from real life, of persons helping young people to feel that people matter. One could quote similar examples from other age-ranges where there is the same concern of individuals for individuals. For however impersonal and ruthless mankind may be in the mass or in individual cases, yet most people can respond to the needs of others with interest and direct service. Man is better than he is sometimes made out to be. Perhaps this is an indication of the divine in human nature—that which the Old Testament writers described as man being made in the image of God. And one of the tasks of Christianity is that of helping man to become what he is capable of becoming—the child of God, the God who cares about people.

LENT

Why pancakes?

Popular customs have a habit of retaining their outward form long after their origin has been forgotten. One example of this is the Shrove Tuesday pancake. It goes back to the mediae-val practice of getting together any butter, fat, sugar or spices left in the larder by that day, and using them up before the next day. This was Ash Wednesday, the beginning of Lent during which Christians abstained from meat, fish, eggs and foods made from milk. Only one meal a day was allowed during this season which was regarded as a solemn period of fasting in preparation for Easter. The discipline became somewhat relaxed later but for centuries the observance of Lent for millions of Christians included alsmgiving, fasting and abstention from all festivities including the solemnisation of matrimony. Nowadays keeping Lent is becoming a matter of personal choice rather than of corporate commitment. The general tendency is also to eliminate those marks which distinguish it from other seasons of the Church's year. Eventually, just as Advent has lost much of its penitential character and become merely the 'weeks before Christmas', so Lent may become the 'weeks before Easter'. Would this be a loss or a gain?

1 Is Lent out of date?

Those who argue that Lent is irrelevant in the modern world, might do so along the following lines:

The traditional expressions and exercises of religious life in the past have little meaning for the spirituality we need today. We think more of service than of self-cultivation, as the heart of religion. Formal and external demonstrations of piety may even be dangerous, as our Lord indicated when he criticised the ostentation of the Pharisees. He advised his followers to fast secretly and pray secretly in the inner chamber rather than in public. He knew that it is dangerously easy for any man to go through the motions of discipline without their having any effect on his character. It may be merely conformity to a group-code. From another angle, we have come to see that extreme forms of self-discipline can be positively harmful not only in suppressing natural instincts but also in engendering deadly pride in one's efforts. Surely in the corporate life of the church, we need to be joyous and thankful, saying 'yes' to life, and not giving the impression of puritanical negativism.

2 *The other side of Lent*

There is some measure of truth in these arguments. They challenge our traditional ideas and practices in Lent. They make us look honestly and objectively at what we do and what we achieve in the practice of our religion. Most of us form habits of praying, or not praying, of communion, or non-communion, and the like. We rarely ask if these habits bear any spiritual fruit even for ourselves, let alone for others who live alongside us. In this most personal realm of our religion, we are reluctant to change or to grow. So our 'spirituality', if that is the word for it, tends to remain static.

It can in fact weaken to the point of complete disappearance if we subscribe to the kind of argument set out above. Its error lies in the assumption that we are so different from our predecessors, so much less external in our piety, so much more realistic in our concern with activism, that their way is no longer relevant to us.

But we may be wrong in our assessment of our own situation. It is one which makes just as many—perhaps even more— demands upon character and spiritual resources than in the past. The stresses and strains of modern life, its insecurity and moral uncertainty, can drain our physical and mental strength. But they also exhaust the reserves of personality so that our very integrity is threatened and life itself loses meaning and purpose. Paul understood the situation all too well. That was why he appealed to the Ephesians to recognise it as a battle against evil requiring the armour of faith and truth, the sword of the Spirit and prayer. In I Corinthians 9 he calls for training and self-discipline for the fulfilment of love and obedience to God. So the object of Lenten discipline can be seen as enabling one not only to meet the pressures of life but to be of use to God.

As to the form of that training, the traditional ways recognised one important fact of life, namely that the body and mind are inseparable. 'Higher thinking' is not much use unless the body is also involved. The control of appetites and of habits of mind go together. Moreover, the new understanding of the mutual sustaining given by members of a group shows the value of individuals getting together and sharing a common purpose and endeavour. So we might do well to think afresh about fasting, almsgiving, study, service and worship together in the common life of the Church. The individual needs to do his training in company, as a member of the Body of Christ.

3 A time of shriving

We described Shrove Tuesday as the day of using up the sweet things before the Lenten fast began. It was often the last day of the season of Carnival (that word means literally 'taking away meat'). But the other feature of this day was the shriving. That was the confession and absolution of the faithful. Before going into the period of training the 'spiritual athlete' needed to be freed from the burden of sin. However simplistic this idea may seem to be, it bears a deep truth. For no amount of personal disciplines or corporate effort will be effective unless it begins at the heart of the personality. For it is there that the issues of good and evil, and the conflicts of will and emotion, have to be fought out. It is there that God's absolution has to be brought to bear to eliminate the roots of the sin that can vitiate our best attempts to achieve renewal. And for that to be effective, requires an honesty which is greater, as James wrote in his Epistle, than that of the man who takes but a fleeting glance at himself in the mirror of life. It is plain common sense.

4 *What sins?*

When the disciples asked Jesus for guidance in prayer, he gave them the Lord's Prayer. When we want guidance in examining our sins, we can turn to the same prayer, not least because of one particular aspect of it: it is the prayer of the *present tense*. There is not a past or a future tense in the whole prayer. In it we ask God to forgive us our trespasses. Not only those we have committed in the past and about which we can do nothing but regret, but those which we are committing even now—and these are by far the most important. They are also the hardest to recognise for they are the sins of thought and word and deed, of attitude and relationship, to which we have become so accustomed that we are hardly aware of them. The Publican in the Temple said: 'God be merciful to me, a sinner.' Christ said that this man in his humility was the justified one. Sometimes the Church appears to convert Publicans into Pharisees, not least in giving them the idea that their sins belong to the past rather than to the present. Yet is is the confession of our present sins that really matters and it is to stop committing them that we must have the good sense and the humility to ask God for his forgiveness and his grace. If we are not ourselves aware of them, then those who have to live with us are often painfully conscious of them. If only, in Paul's words, we could know 'as we have been known . . . ' but perhaps that would be too much to bear.

So in Lent we are not called upon to fill in a questionnaire about our past, or to undergo a psychological analysis to identify those whom we can blame for our personal problems. Instead we are asked to face the truth about ourselves with repentance, but also with hope. Then Lent—and the word means literally 'Spring'—can be for us a season of positive growth and joyous preparation for the renewal of life which is the Easter gift of the Risen Lord.

LENT

The Way of Christ

The trouble with most temptations is that they seem so reasonable. It was so with those which faced Jesus in the wilderness. Each of them looked so sensible in respect both of his own mission and of the people for whom it was intended.

To turn stone into bread was harmless enough. To do his work properly, a prophet had to look after his physical needs. If he had means whereby to provide for the hungry, then surely it was his duty to use them. That descent from the pinnacle—perhaps it was something of a gimmick. But it was an effective method of commanding attention for his message. Then there was the suggestion of using power to win the world. Think of the millions of oppressed people, nations living in fear and conflict, the threat to civilisation itself from barbarian hordes ready to destroy law and order. So much trouble and bloodshed would be avoided by establishing God's kingdom by the right use of power. Men would be happy and secure and then surely they would be willing to accept Christianity.

Jesus rejected all three. Their advantage would be short-term and superficial. They appealed to man's lower nature and made no demands upon him. They were not according to God's will. Each of them was theologically unsound. One ignored the fact that man's basic need is spiritual and not material. The second subjected God to testing. The third denied the priority of allegiance to God.

But simply to reject them would have been a merely negative response. Jesus had a positive alternative and that was the Way he chose.

1 Method and mission

The Gospels do not attempt to offer a chronological framework into which we can fit events in detailed sequence. Instead they show us a few main developments. Jesus began where people were already, within the framework of law and synagogue. He went deeper than the letter of the law and the accretions of rabbinic exposition, to seek the will of God behind the law. He asked fundamental questions about the nature of God and nature of man.

His behaviour was in the old prophetic tradition, for the revival of which the people longed. There were works of healing which he did more out of compassion than to attract attention to his mission. Most important was his preaching to the poor, as he showed the Baptist's disciples. He was not aiming at mass conversions and withdrew whenever it looked as though the multitude was going to respond by making him the spearhead of social or religious revolution. He would not engage in power-politics, nor in deliberate confrontation with the religious establishment, until this became inevitable. He confined his mission mainly to people of his own race. Yet he did not reject the response of faith when made by Gentiles.

His method seemed at first to be one customary among Jewish Rabbis. This was to gather round the teacher a small band of devoted disciples. But the difference was that they were being trained for action after his departure. So for a period of about two years he lived with them, giving them increasingly demanding teaching. He entrusted them with a mission of their own, sent out in pairs. Finally, after the Resurrection, he left them to manage on their own but in his spiritual strength and with the guidance of the Holy Spirit. They had to learn that their way, and his, was that of the Cross, the sign of suffering but also of victory.

2 No other way

Many religions have been founded on other ways both of approaching God and of meeting human needs. Some have been concerned to perfect man's soul by liberating it from the imperfections of the world. Others have presented religion as a way of strict conformity to moral and ritual rules. For some, personal self-fulfilment has been the goal. For others it has been mystical union with the divine. Nowadays we value the particular and positive contributions of non-Christian religions more sympathetically than in times past. We realise that God in his infinite wisdom has made himself known to men in many ways.

But there were aspects of the Way of Christ which made it unique. One was the freedom to respond or to reject, which it accepted as essential to human integrity. Another was the double dimension of relationship with both God and other men, which it regarded as inseparable. A third was the attention paid to inward motivation even more than to outward conduct. An important aspect of Christ's teaching was its ability to hold together in creative tension concepts which seemed diverse. For example, he called for detachment from the world but at the same time for compassionate involvement in it. Another example was his emphasis on the need for the response of faith along with the offer of God's free grace.

The unique element in Christianity was of course the Incarnation of the Son of God, who came into the world because of God's love for it. By his life and death he atoned for it and reconciled it to God. He rose again for the sake of humanity. This is the cardinal truth of the Gospel and everything hinges upon it. For if this is not true, then Christianity is simply a form of idealism. If the Church is not based upon it, then it is simply a man-made society for mutual welfare.

It took some time for the first Christians to understand this fact of the Incarnation. They did so only when they had had time to reflect upon their experience of Jesus during his lifetime, and upon their awareness of his continuing presence with them since the Resurrection. They realised that his had been the Way of the Incarnate Son of God. They saw too that theirs must be the Way of the Body of Christ.

3 The way ahead

It is interesting that one of the very earliest names for Christianity was The Way. This implied something more than a sect or a society. It stood for a manner of life and a movement of spirit, in which people grew together as they responded to changing circumstances and new opportunities. It would have been understandable if, faced as it was by Jewish and Gentile hostility, the Church had drawn in upon itself and become static. Instead, it went out into the world presenting Jesus, in his own words, as the way, the truth and the life. All three of these were living and dynamic realities.

This suggests that Christianity should be presented in the same terms in our own age, which once again presents a missionary situation. A generation which has lost its way has little sense of direction and purpose. Plans and policies have not produced happiness or security. Man has achieved a substantial mastery of his environment, but not of himself. He needs to find, not a way of by-passing his problems, but one which will take him through them to achieve real progress and peace of mind. Advice is of little use to him. He wants to see the way demonstrated by people who share his situation and his problems, who have come to terms with insecurity but have found a real security in the power of God.

So the Church has to show itself to be a fellowship with a purpose. It also has to be a pilgrimage which proclaims the truth, again as a living reality. The Christian Gospel is in one sense constant and eternal: 'the faith which was once for all delivered to the saints.' But in another sense it is continuously and excitingly being discovered as Christians learn more and more about the activity of God in the Church and in the world. This, after all, is one way in which Jesus fulfils his promise of the guidance of the Spirit.

The way and the truth—and the life. The Christian believes that life is worth living. He says 'Yes' to life because he says 'Yes' to God. The two positive affirmations go together, as they did throughout the life of Christ. As with our Lord, they may mean the acceptance of suffering and of costly and compassionate involvement in the troubles of humanity. But this was the way he chose, rejecting the three temptations which dominate the world today—the temptations of materialism, of superficiality and of the abuse of power. He knew that he could bring men to the Kingdom of God only by living with them, loving them and dying for them.

LENT

The mind of Christ

When King Saul hurled a spear at David as he played the lyre, the action was neither a musical criticism nor a sudden impulse. It was the culmination of months of jealous brooding over the success of his young protegé of whom the people sang:

> 'Saul has slain his thousands
> And David his ten thousands.'

Saul was suffering from something which the Old Testament describes as 'evil imagination' which could destroy personality and relationships. Many of its writers had taught that religion was a matter of the inward disposition even more than of outward behaviour. The Great Commandment itself had emphasised this, requiring that man should love God with all his heart, soul and mind and—only lastly—with all his strength. The prophets took up the same theme. Micah put the love of kindness and humility alongside doing justice as constituting what God required of those who would serve him. At a time of national upheaval, Isaiah could affirm: 'Thou wilt keep him in perfect peace whose mind is stayed on thee.'

1 *Mind in the Gospel*

The same emphasis is continued in the New Testament even if the terms used do not quite correspond with modern definitions of mind and heart and soul. Man is thought of as one whole person, body and mind and spirit. But religion was tending to lay overmuch emphasis on the external side of behaviour, in respect both of goodness and sin. That was why, according to Mark 7.14-23, Jesus had to challenge the conventional view that defilement came from contact with things that were ritually unclean. He declared that it arose from what came out of a man. It was his thinking that produced 'fornication, theft, murder, adultery, coveting, wickedness, deceit, licentiousness, envy, pride and foolishness'. Even temptation would not necessarily defile until the mind had succumbed to it.

Jesus' understanding of the relation between body and mind may be illustrated by his cure of the young paralysed man brought to him by his friends. There, without laying hands on the patient, Jesus went to the root of his condition by declaring that he was forgiven. As so often happens, here was one whose disease of the mind manifested itself in a disease of the body. He needed a psychosomatic, or mind-body, treatment.

Matthew 6.25 offers an interesting example of another side of our Lord's understanding of the mind. The command is translated as 'Take no thought for your life. . . ' or 'Be not anxious'. But the verb *merimnao* means to be split-minded and this accurately describes the root cause of much anxiety and worry. Jesus frequently commends the single-mindedness of complete and integrated devotion to God. One cannot serve two masters. So the believer must be completely detached from that slavery to possessions which is a kind of idolatry.

2 The mind of Paul

Paul wrote about the mind on a number of occasions. Writing to the Philippians about the danger of rivalry and self-interest, he gave us the magnificent passage in which he dared to say: 'Let this mind be in you which was also in Christ Jesus . . . ' If Christianity is the imitation of Christ then this is more than a matter of outward behaviour. Its keynote is humility in the mind.

But this is easier said than done. In Galatians 5, Paul spoke of the conflict between the lower and the higher natures. Modern psychology might question the distinction by which so many vices, from immorality to sorcery and carousing, are attributed to the lower and fleshly nature which must be crucified by those who would belong to Christ. Paul's main point was that when the Spirit is allowed to work freely in the mind, its fruits are evident and lasting. And in Philippians 4, he encouraged men to make the effort to think positively about things which are true, honourable, just, pure, lovely, gracious, excellent and worthy of praise.

Nevertheless the Apostle spoke from his own experience of the conflict between good and evil in the mind of man. In Romans 7.15-25, he admitted that he could will to do right and yet fail to achieve it. He could will not to do evil and still find himself lapsing into it. Only Christ could deliver him from this paralysis of personality.

But how could this deliverance be made effective? The answer lay in a word which occurs only once in the entire New Testament. It is in Colossians 3.15: 'Let the peace of Christ rule in your hearts.' The word translated 'rule' literally means 'arbitrate'. Paul's image was of Christ, the giver of peace and unity in the mind, helping a man to decide between different courses of action and conflicting priorities. It is like a man in doubt asking seriously the question: 'What is Christ saying about the matter?' and accepting the answer.

3 What do you think?

This question of the unity of personality was very evident also in the teaching of John the beloved disciple. In 1 John 4.18 he wrote of living within the love of God, the love which casts out the fear that sours life. But he emphasised that no man can claim to love God while he hates his brother. To do so is not only a kind of hypocrisy but it also splits the personality. This is worth remembering when we find it hard to love God, for this may be because in another part of the mind we are nursing bitterness towards someone else.

Psychology has helped us to recognise that our thinking is not as straightforward and independent as we would like to believe it to be. The experience of our childhood and upbringing is active in the unconscious depths of our personalities. We have also absorbed the ideas and values, the goals and the fears of our human environment. Our consciences are an imperfect guide, under-educated as they are. We need the humility and the sense to recognise these factors affecting our freedom of choice and decisions.

But even when we come nearer to facing the truth about ourselves, we need something more to be able to do something about it. Diagnosis is not sufficient. The treatment has to come from two directions. One is the outreach of the personality towards God in faith. The other is the grace of God which cleanses, strengthens and renews. This is what Paul called the transformation of the mind—not a spiritual dry-cleaning but a complete re-direction of it. And he believed that then the peace of God which passed all human understanding would keep men's hearts and minds in Christ Jesus.

It was Plato who wrote that the soul is dyed the colour of its thoughts. It is only sensible to ask ourselves what is the colour of our own thinking, about ourselves, our loved ones, our work, our play, our friends and those who differ from us. What do we think about our own lives and what have we done so far with them? What about suffering and what about death? Our dreams and our worries, our secret temptations—perhaps they are not as hidden as we imagine them to be. We reveal them unconsciously in our gestures and mannerisms, in our reaction to anything which stimulates our prejudices or brings us joy. And this is what happens when the world looks at a Christian and hopes to see that in his heart he is a man who has the mind of Christ, the peace of God and the fruit of the Spirit.

LENT

Lord, teach us to pray

John the Baptist was a man of action, fiercely critical of corruption, energetically appealing to men to repent while there was still time. But there was another side to his ministry. John was a man of prayer and in this he also trained his disciples. So when he sent them to follow Jesus, they asked him to teach them to pray. The request is a little surprising. They were Jews accustomed to praying daily at the third, sixth and ninth hours. They were accustomed to services in the synagogue in which prayer figured prominently. But they quickly came to recognise that there was something outside their experience in the form, content and manner of prayer as Jesus offered it. They knew that he often went away on his own to be quiet with God. They knew that he prayed for them corporately and individually. They saw him praying on many occasions of particular importance such as his baptism, at the call of the disciples, and the transfiguration. He would do so again in the agony of Gethsemane and Calvary. Jesus appeared to do nothng without prayer and it accompanied many of his miracles.

He taught them that it should be offered humbly, earnestly and persistently even if at first it did not appear to be answered. It must be simple and unostentatious. The forgiveness of others was an essential pre-requisite. So too was complete faith and trust in God. The Fourth Gospel records that he taught them to make their requests in his name. This would carry the implication that they should ask only what could rightly be asked for in the name of Jesus.

1 *The church at prayer*

These simple but profound rules were carried out by the early Church which 'devoted itself to prayer' immediately after the Ascension. It accompanied all times of decision such as the appointment of Matthias, and when they were doing works of healing. When one of their number was in trouble, as for example when Peter was in prison, they prayed together for long periods. Corporate prayer became very important to them and the apostolic writers saw this as the realm in which the Holy Spirit gave them powerful assistance. The writer of the Epistle to the Hebrews saw the present work of Jesus in heaven as interceding on their behalf. And the New Testament ends with a prayer for his return. The life of the Church depended on prayer, lived in it and grew in it. This was an essential part of The Way.

2 *The range of prayer*

We are inclined to think of prayer as a spiritual exercise of personal religion. The New Testament stresses its corporate aspect. It is noteworthy that when Jesus was asked to teach his disciples, he put the Lord's Prayer in the plural and not the singular. He did not say: 'My father . . . give me this day my daily bread . . . forgive me my trespasses . . . lead me not into temptation . . . deliver me from evil.'

We continue this in our corporate worship but it is worth asking what relation there is between our praying corporately and praying individually. They are not separate and unrelated activities. The corporate experience should be helping the individual, teaching him about the nature of prayer, broadening its vocabulary and widening its context. So we look at the prayer life of the local church to which we belong. The words of its liturgy may be superb but by themselves they can become over-familiar and so remote from everyday life as to be almost anaesthetic in their effect. The language of liturgy is not meant to supply solely aesthetic satisfaction. It is fair to ask what real meaning we give to corporate confession and acts of penitence, and if in our intercessions we are trying to bring before God the real needs of the world.

It is reasonable to inquire if our corporate prayer is really corporate in the sense of bringing together the whole body of Christians in that place. The early Christians prayed for each other constantly. The modern Christian tends to pray in church for his brethren only when they are ill. But people are in need of the support of their fellows when they are well, facing problems and responsibilities, taking up a new job, or battling with economic problems. Those of us who are clergy and ministers know what a difference it makes to us to know that our congregation is praying for us. One is reminded of the cogent comment 'No one is entitled to criticise the sermon who has not prayed for the preacher!' And within the organisations of the church, many a conflict or argument might be tackled differently if the meeting began with real prayer and not with a kind of brief nod in the direction of heaven. For sincere prayer does change relations between the people praying, even in committees.

3 *Prayer is communion*

If corporate praying is a communion between persons, private prayer should be a communion with God. This is a two-way relation reaching out from both sides, listening and speaking, a conversation between friends responding to each other. If ours is the continuing 'practice of the presence of God', then at a time of crisis we do not find ourselves attempting to establish an unfamiliar contact.

That is not to say that for those who are accustomed to living in God's presence, prayer is necessarily easy. Many of the biographies of saints speak of times when they found it hard. It was often difficult to accept the will of God, to fight against temptations, to accept suffering, to pray for their persecutors. They went through dry periods when religion itself became wearisome or endured dark nights of desolation. They were not immune to the worries, the depression or the loneliness which can beset any of us. But they faced these situations openly and prayed their way through them.

Their praying was also characterised by an honesty which most of us find it hard to achieve. Even on his knees and in solitude it can be as hard for a man to be honest with himself as when he is with others. He may be prepared to bring before God all his problems except the one which matters most. His assessment is liable to be clouded by self-pity and self-excusing or by a somewhat complacent comparison of himself with others. In the long run, man's main problem is to live with himself as he really is. This is where prayer can let God's grace get to work if we open our hearts and minds to it. We have to accept God's forgiveness without which we cannot forgive ourselves even if this means admitting that the sins which we condemn so vehemently in others are those to which we are secretly drawn, and the reason why we hate others is because secretly we hate ourselves. For in prayer, where there is honesty, there is hope.

4 *To whom we pray*

The Lord's Prayer starts with God. Most of us begin our praying, with ourselves. Whether we begin or end with him, God is the one to whom we pray and who can do something about the object of our prayer. The Psalmist wrote: 'Be still, and know that I am God.' The Hebrew word for 'be still' means *'let go'*—a sermon in itself! This is not passive relaxing of mind and spirit, but surrender to God's presence. Nowadays it has become fashionable to talk about 'transcendental meditation' although there is nothing strictly transcendental about an exercise in detachment. Prayer has direction and communion and variety. Adoration, thanksgiving, intercession, confession, meditation—there are so many ways of praying and yet they are all part of this movement of the soul to God. And its fruit is not just peace of mind, reconciliation to others, strength in trial or hope in darkness. It is all these and more. It is the consecration of life itself to God. For the last word of Jesus on the Cross was the crown of all his praying: 'Father, into thy hands I commend my spirit.'

LENT

What price motherhood?

The Bible is never dewy-eyed about human nature, not even about motherhood. Many of the mothers of the Old Testament are formidable characters, playing important parts in the drama of Israel. Among the patriarchal families there is Sarah, jealously protecting her son Isaac and ruthlessly driving out into the wilderness her handmaid Hagar and the child Ishmael. Then in the family of Isaac there develops one of those dangerous 'family favourites' situations. Jacob is the apple of his mother's eye. He is neat and tidy about the house. His brother

Esau is the wild one, sporty and tough and beloved of his father. Rebecca has no scruples about deceiving her aged husband even though the result is disastrous to everyone concerned. The later history of the nation was influenced by another powerful mother, Bathsheba. She manipulated a palace revolution and deceived her husband David to win the throne for her son Solomon. In the long run this led to the division of the nation.

There is another side to the record. We have the greatest mother-in-law in the Bible in Naomi. She won the love of her foreign daughter-in-law Ruth and brought her back to find a second husband in Israel. This was to establish the line which led to David himself. Then there is Hannah, mother of Samuel. When her prayers were answered, she kept her side of the covenant. She dedicated her infant son to the service of God and was content to see him once a year, bringing him 'a little robe' each time. The boy grew up unscathed by the religious corruption at Shiloh, to be the first of the prophetic founders of the nation.

1 *Mothers of the Gospel*

The mothers of the New Testament tend to make their contribution quietly in the background. When the mothers of the disciples saw their sons throwing up the security of their jobs to follow Jesus, they must have been deeply concerned. The anxiety of many must have been represented by the concern expressed by Zebedee's wife. She tried to get Jesus to promise that her two sons, James and John, would have positions of importance in the Kingdom. But he gently refused to be committed.

We have to forget the stained-glass-window pictures of the disciples as aged and venerable saints, and remember that they were a band of young men. As they wandered around Palestine, someone must have helped them from time to time with food and accommodation, and done their washing and mending for them. We have rare glimpses of households where Jesus and the Twelve could find such welcome help. Finally, at the

Cross there were the mothers whose devotion outweighed any fear of rough handling from the soldiers or abuse from the crowd.

Among them was Mary. Like Elizabeth with the Baptist, Mary gave no sign throughout her son's ministry of wanting to interfere with what he was doing. Yet it must have been tempting to do so. He appeared to be setting himself against the 'Establishment' and causing scandal by his attitude to the Sabbath. There is only one incident when it was reported to Jesus that his mother and brothers wanted to talk to him. Our Lord replied that whoever did the will of God was his brother and sister and mother. A hard saying? But it was only consonant with Christ's teaching about the whole family of the children of the Father. Moreover, it was in line with his teaching that the service of God must over-ride the traditional claims of family life. This included even the duty of attending to the burial of one's father. To Christ even the family was not the highest and most absolute of relationships. Nevertheless within it the responsibilities of caring and protection remained. In his last moments on the Cross, Jesus was concerned to provide a home for his mother, for whom old Simeon's prophecy was being tragically fulfilled.

2 Even motherhood has changed

This generation has seen a revolution in the attitude towards motherhood. On the good side, there is a welcome emphasis on the sharing of responsibility between fathers and mothers in the upbringing of their children. The welfare state has given some measure of support to motherhood. Family planning has made it possible to lessen the strain of the constant child-bearing of the past, and to have only the number of children who can be brought up 'properly'. The content of that adverb varies from one class and group to another, according to the ideas and standards of individual families—and their willingness to give priority to parenthood.

But there is another side to all this. Economic pressures and changing ideas of material and social priorities have somewhat displaced the former assumption that parenthood was the natural consequence of marriage. Insecurity in marriage relationships, in place of the security of mutual commitment, tends to discourage bringing children into the world. Contraception and even abortion have ceased to have the same moral overtones they had in the past. If a marriage is in difficulties, then the children are thought of more as a problem than as a reason for the parents staying together. And now we have the comparatively new phenomenon of thousands of single-parent families which can often but not always present acute problems for the parent and the children concerned. The pattern of motherhood and family life is also being radically changed by the extension of full-time employment of mothers.

3 What next?

In 1885, at a Church Congress in Portsmouth, a country parson's wife reluctantly agreed to speak to a vast audience of women. She said:

'At the present moment the eyes of England are directed in a very special manner upon the women. It is said that there is in many cases a terrible want of morality and high tone in the homes and among the people of this country and the question is *What can be done to raise the national character?* The answer is, *Let us appeal to the mothers of England.* It is the mothers who can in great measure work the reformation of the country.'

That woman was Mary Sumner, the founder of the Mothers' Union. In her own life as a mother there were two outstanding principles. One was 'Be yourself what you wish your children to be'. The other was 'Prayer is the unseen power that moves mountains'. And far from being a patronising socialite 'doing good' to the poorer classes, Mary Sumner dared to insist that 'Educated women need the Mothers' Union and its clear firm principles much more than mothers of the poorer classes'. In common with her friend the great reformer Josephine Butler, who was also a parson's wife, Mary Sumner dared in those Victorian days to affirm the principle of high and equal moral standards for men and women alike. Theirs was a vision not only of motherhood but also of womanhood itself with a new realism.

4 *Mothering Sunday*

When the Church celebrates each year its Mothering Sunday, it has to do so in equally realistic terms, far removed from the commercialised glamour of 'Mother's Day'. This Sunday began with an act of gratitude to the Church which is in a real sense 'the mother of us all', and the source of true liberty. This is how the Epistle describes it. The keynote of this commemoration is gratitude, not least to our mothers for all their love and devotion and self-sacrifice. And mothers—and fathers too—get little enough gratitude and encouragement from the community as a whole these days.

The day sounds a call to the liberation of women, of men and of children, from the pressures of a world which would dehumanise them and ignore their basic need of the essential liberty to be the children of God their Father. And the bulwark of that freedom, where its nature can be discovered and its use developed, is still in the home.

LENT

The face of violence

One of the most baffling phenomena of contemporary life is the rapid spread of violence. Every year, police reports record increases in crimes of violence, committed even by children. Muggings, battering of wives and babies, and savage attacks on old people, are frequently in the news. So is vandalism and apparently meaningless destruction of property. In every continent violence appears to be the inevitable accompaniment of protest, whether it is industrial, political or social. It permeates the visual arts and, even more significantly, the powerful medium of television. It influences what people say as well as what they do. For the language in which people express themselves seems to have become more violent than heretofore.

This happens at every level of the community. Swearing and the use of what used to be regarded as vulgar expressions are taken for granted with little comment. The counsel of the Delphic Oracle: 'Moderation in all things', belongs to a forgotten world.

1 *The roots of violence*

The causes of violence, like those of war, are deep rooted and complex. It often arises from a conflict within the personality in which the defects of upbringing are stimulated by fear, frustration or insecurity. A man may react violently against someone else when in reality he is demonstrating against something within himself. This was how Paul behaved. Persecuting the Christians, he was in fact kicking against the pricks of the challenge of Stephen's death. Even towards those whom one loves, one can behave cruelly because of some inner tension. It is disturbing that affection and maturity, and even the veneer of 'civilisation', seem to be so vulnerable to inward pressures.

There would appear to be external pressures, also, which produce this kind of situation. Man has produced an environment of material and physical security which should encourage stability. Yet he creates within it a prison of meaninglessness. Its impersonality threatens his sense of values and makes him feel helpless. Violence is his way of making significant protest.

This is particularly true when he is compelled to live in so large a mass of people that he is unable to find meaning in his social environment. We see this in the inner cities. They have shown a marked impoverishment in the last decade. Those who still live in them may suffer from a multiple deprivation in terms of housing, education, employment and social services. The failure of our cities is a failure of our whole society.

Yet the problem can recur in the vast new housing estate. Its very size impedes the development of a feeling of being a community in which the individual or the family can put down roots and make effective contacts. So loneliness and withdrawal, vandalism and violence, may be found even in the new areas. But these factors while helping to engender violence do not in themselves produce it. For it is the response of an individual that counts. The external influence upon it is secondary. But both sides of the problem have to be understood before any one can make judgements about behaviour problems. We have to get clear in our minds, also, what kind of a society we have produced, and what kind of society we want. To achieve it, may require action which would be so positive and far-reaching as to seem almost 'violent' to those who favour a policy of *laissez faire*.

2 *Active or passive?*

The Gospel reflects one aspect of this problem which is of contemporary significance. This is the question of the use of force in a right cause when no other means of reform appears to be possible. Those who think of our Lord only as 'Gentle Jesus, meek and mild' ignore his behaviour when he cleansed the Temple. The scourging and the upsetting of the tables was as deliberate as it was effective. There is no doubt that Jesus was regarded by his enemies as a man of violence, not so much in respect of his deeds as of his teaching.

It is clear that both in that age and later the world came to consider his religion of peace and love as highly dangerous. It was seen as a challenge to structures of government and to their methods of keeping law and order. The Epistles to the Romans and to Titus, and Peter, show apostolic sensitivity to this suspicion and advise their readers to do nothing to deserve it.

But inevitably Christianity was forced into situations of confrontation. Mediaeval theologians argued about the possibility of Christians having to engage in a 'just war' against oppression and evil. This question does no belong solely to the past. It can face us today when religion is caught up in a struggle for freedom and justice. There can come a point at which violent action seem to be the only way of resisting evil and defending human values. If, however, Christians believe that they must adhere to a principle of passive resistance, then they may have to pay a price for this, not least that of being misunderstood by the world.

3 Is there an answer?

Our society is realising that there is little use in meeting violence by violence. It can be as ineffective as trying to eliminate crime by increasing deterrents and punishments. To be effective, any action—whether legislative, social, educational or religious—has to be based upon patient and competent analysis of the causes of violence in man's social environment and in his own personality. This includes the recognition that in place of strife, man is really asking for security and affection, not necessarily for a life of ease but for one of meaning for himself and his family and, in a sense, for humanity itself.

That is why it is not a religious 'bromide' to suggest that the answer to violence is salvation. For by salvation the Gospel means wholeness. It may have to begin with a man's reconciliation to himself as well as to his neighbours. Essentially, it means accepting that reconciliation to God which was the work of Christ for all men. This is the response of faith to the love of God. And, again, this is not a theological platitude. For the problem of violence is basically a problem of faith.

Christ believed that men were capable of making the response of faith. When he was hanging on a cross by the side of Jesus, one man of violence did so, though the other refused. The witness of those who accept the way of reconciliation is nevertheless a powerful influence in any generation. They are saying that their neighbours are human beings like themselves, to be respected as persons but not to be feared as threats. They refuse to let themselves be overwhelmed by the forces within and without which might impel them to strike out blindly against others. They are prepared to accept suffering with patience and with hope. And they are willing to accept the hardest role of all, that of the mediator, to try to reconcile men even when they are at their most violent. For this they are more likely to receive a cross than a crown. But Jesus singled them out for a particular blessing as the 'sons of God'.

Saint Francis prayed: 'Merciful God, to thee we commend ourselves, and all those who need thy help and correction. Where there is hatred, give love; where there is injury, pardon; where there is doubt, faith; where there is despair, hope; where there is sadness, joy; where there is darkness, light. Grant that we may not seek so much to be consoled as to console; to be understood, as to understand; to be loved, as to love; For in giving we receive, in pardoning we are pardoned, and dying we are born into eternal life.'

HOLY WEEK

Mountains of the Bible

The Bible is never sentimental about mountains. When the Psalmist wrote: 'I will lift up mine eyes unto the hills from whence cometh my help,' he was not thinking of the hills as the source of strength, but of the Lord who had created them. The whole psalm is a 'Song of Ascents'. It would have been part of the annual ritual of procession from the Women's Court up the steps to the men's area of the Temple. Its aim was to glorify, as the keeper and protector who neither 'slumbers nor sleeps', the Lord on high.

Mountains and hills are prominent in the story of the Old Testament. When the Israelites came into the Promised Land, they found themselves faced with a developed civilisation. The religious cultus emphasised the nature-cycle. Its most prominent features were the 'high places' on the hill tops, with their upright pillar and prostrate altar. The worship had strongly sexual connotations and there might also be human sacrifice. It was dangerously easy for the immigrants to believe that this kind of religion was necessary to sustain the agricultural processes. They would wonder if the God who had guided them through the wilderness was effective in the new situation. And long after the tribes were settled and united, the old high places had their attractiveness. The hill top and the mountain could be a battle ground of faith.

1 *The place of decision*

Time after time the Jews had to be reminded of another mountain, Sinai. It had been the most holy place which no ordinary mortal could presume to climb, save Moses to whom God had revealed himself. Here they had been given the Law, and the Covenant between the Almighty and his Chosen People had been established. It had been the place of revelation and of testing.

The same was evident in another dramatic scene, this time at Carmel. There Elijah confronted the full strength of Baalism supported by the royal house. He was overwhelmingly victorious. But when his life was threatened by Jezebel, Elijah despaired and fled to Mount Horeb. There he was given a revelation of God not through the wind, earthquake or fire, but in a 'still, small voice'. Elijah was given his commission to eliminate the religion of Baal, to raise the moral level of Israel and so to begin the Prophetic Revolution.

2 *Mountains of the Gospel*

The modern pilgrim in the Holy Land finds that whatever changes time may have brought to the valleys and towns, the mountains have been little affected. It is not difficult there to recall scenes of some of the most important events of the Gospel. From Jericho's orange groves one can look across the Jordan valley to the grim mountain scarp of the Wilderness. There Jesus was tested as he meditated on the ends and means of his mission. One goes up into the mountains past the Inn of the Good Samaritan, then through Bethany and eventually to the Mount of Olives. There Jesus beheld the city down across the valley, and wept over it. And it was there that he ascended, taking leave of his disciples for the last time.

One goes northward along the Lake of Galilee to the Mountain of the Beatitudes where Jesus preached to the Multitude. The writer of the Gospel according to Matthew assembles the material of the Sermon in such a way as to present it as the new Law-Giving, recalling the revelation of Sinai.

Still further north, one comes to the scene of the Transfiguration whether this was the traditional site of Mount Tabor or the more probable location nearer Caesarea Philippi, on a spur of the Hermon range. In some ways the mountain of the Transfiguration was the most significant of all. Here, a week after Jesus had clearly prophesied his coming Passion, that mysterious event took place which only Peter, James and John witnessed. Luke records that Jesus spoke about his 'exodus' with Moses and Elijah—those two previous recipients of mountain-revelations. A voice was heard acknowledging his divine sonship. Using the familiar imagery of the Feast of Tabernacles, Peter suggested that booths should be made for this inspiring experience to continue. But Jesus and the three disciples had to leave the mountain top and return to the valley.

There they found the other disciples dismayed by their failure to cure an epileptic boy. And Jesus had to tell them that they were lacking in faith. From the heights of Transfiguration, Jesus and his companions had come down to the human problems of suffering and failure. He healed the lad and, Luke adds significantly, 'all were astonished at the majesty of God'.

3 Height and depth

The story of the Transfiguration and its epilogue, is a kind of parable of the incarnation, a drama of the sacramental principle. Every one of us needs at times to get away to the spiritual experience of the mountain top. As Wordsworth wrote:

> 'The world is too much with us; late and soon,
> Getting and spending, we lay waste our powers.'

The Christian can make the mistake of trying to keep going without the times of quiet and prayer, of recollection and reflection when he can detach himself from his busyness to think about life as a whole. Perhaps he needs to give some thought to the purpose of his life, and to weigh up as Jesus did, his priorities and how to achieve them. He can wait upon God as Moses did, to discover what may be the Father's will for him and to renew his covenant with God.

This is something much more positive and purposeful than the attempt to 'get away from it all' which is rarely successful, because it tends to be negative and aimless. We may succeed in getting away from busyness and routine. But we have not succeeded in getting away from ourselves. The answer is to accept that fact and bring ourselves into the presence of God so that with his help we can look at our whole manner of life from that spiritual mountain top. This is epitomised in the Lord's Prayer itself. It begins with two words which are not simply a statement of faith but sum up the profound experience of union with Our Father. Perhaps we are all too familiar with this prayer for this aspect of it to be readily apparent. But whenever we may be able to snatch a moment of quiet, we could simply repeat to ourselves the two words 'Our Father' and let them be the centre of our thoughts and prayers. Then two things begin to happen. One is that the presence of God becomes more real to us, before we go on to make the rest of our petitions.

The other is that like the three disciples we move from the mountain to the valley. For he is *Our* Father and we have to share his love with others. That is one of the great Christian truths, almost a platitude perhaps, but its challenge can confront us as it did the disciples when we return from prayer and worship to the workaday world. We have prayed for humility, and find ourselves humiliated. We have prayed for peace in our souls, and we have to hold on to it in a situation of conflict. We have asked for patience and we are thrust into a situation where we can easily become irritated and exasperated. We have prayed for God to give us a task, and we have to clean up the mess left by the selfishness of others. We have longed to experience the presence of Jesus, and we have to recognise him coming to us disguised as a fellow human being in need.

When Peter and James and John came down from the mountain, they found their fellow disciples in a situation of failure and embarrassment. But the three companions of Jesus had had a unique experience which had brought them nearer to understanding the divinity of their Master. They were to see the divinity and the humanity at one in a work of healing, bringing wholeness to a broken life and mastering the power of evil. They were also to hear Jesus give his disciples the firm assurance of the infinite power of faith.

The whole story of the Transfiguration and what followed it, is one of profound joy. Yet it is not the joy of a happy interlude providing a temporary relief from the drama of the Gospel narrative. It is the keynote of all that led up to the Passion. For here is the assurance of the nature of God incarnate in his Son, the certainty that what lay ahead was not a tragic accident but the expression of the divine purpose. It was once again proof that the love of God could be brought to bear on every problem. Christ had been transfigured and so too, in a sense, was every human situation. It was to this revelation that the disciples were called to give the response of faith—and so are we. For whether we know the heights of worship or the depths of suffering, we are there with Christ, who is our Emmanuel—God with us.

HOLY WEEK

A faith for disaster

Suddenly it happens, and thousands die. A flood, volcanic eruption, tidal wave or an earthquake—and the toll in human life and suffering is enormous. The sophisticated world gets a sharp reminder of its vulnerability to the forces of nature. International relief agencies swing into action to an extent which would have been unimaginable a generation ago. For a time animosity and indifference disappear.

But the fact that the calamity happens at all raises questions, not least to men of faith. It asks us if we really care about the sufferings of others and how we prove this. It may also start us wondering about God himself. We may wonder if this vulnerability to natural disaster is part of the price man pays for the freedom which God gives him. Some might suggest that a calamity like this makes nonsense of moral endeavour and prayer, of theology and ethics. In recent years disasters of these kinds have happened mainly to people in far-off lands, on the volcanic belt of the Pacific or the hurricane areas of the Caribbean. If they occurred here in one's own country, the questions might have a different edge to them.

1 *What Jesus said*

The problem is hard enough for us to face, but it was even harder for people of Christ's time. Nowadays few of us give much thought to the question of God's providence as working in and through nature. During the long drought of the summer of 1976, for instance, there was a curious embarrassment in Britain about praying for rain, as if this would be a return to primitive superstition.

But in the first century AD the people of Palestine saw Providence in every event. The seasons, the climate, the movements of the heavenly bodies, were all in the hand of God as were the incidents of personal life. Their historians did not shrink from interpreting even disastrous happenings as due to God's action, as in David's being moved to commit the sin of numbering the people. The early Christians inherited the same belief, so much so that in the Epistle of Saint James, the writer had to counter the idea that even the temptation to do evil could come from God.

If God caused everything and God was just, then there must be some moral justification for a disaster, which presumably lay in the sinfulness of those to whom it happened. This was the argument of Job's 'comforters' which Job indignantly refused, believing himself to be guiltless.

Jesus rejected this conventional argument in a very significant passage in Luke 13. He had been told of some Galileans massacred on Pilate's orders when they were offering sacrifices during worship. His informants assumed that God had let this awful thing happen because of the wickedness of the worshippers. Jesus demanded evidence of this and asked if the men killed had been sinners more than any other Galileans. He quoted the case of eighteen people killed by the fall of a tower in Siloam, down in the valley below the city wall. Were they thought of as offenders worse than anyone else living in Jerusalem? The lessons of these disasters, he urged, was a call to repentance lest spiritual catastrophe should overtake his hearers. Once again he was stressing the need for spiritual preparedness.

2 The greater problem

It would appear that Jesus was much less concerned about natural disasters than about those which men bring upon themselves. The universe which is the context of all life is in itself neutral. When a calamity occurs, it is the human response to it which matters.

Christ concentrated upon the universe of human relationships. It is there that mankind can bring horrors upon itself more far-reaching in their effects than accidents of nature. In our own century, there has been the genocide in which four million Jews were destroyed under Nazi rule. We have seen slaughter in the Lebanon, terrorism in Northern Ireland and the carnage which has accompanied the emergence of new nations. They bear comparison with anything that has happened in previous eras. Evil has triumphed over goodness and humanity itself has been crucified over and over again.

There is a sense in which the death of Jesus was in itself a crucifixion of humanity, destroyed by blind prejudice, fear and hatred. And those responsible for it were ordinary people. Some of them thought it was 'expedient' that one man should die, even if he were innocent. Some were quite sure that what they were doing was justifiable in protection of their religion. Tradition has exaggerated the participants in the trial and execution of Jesus into unreal figures of abnormal wickedness. The fact is that there was a devastating ordinariness about them. We meet all the figures of the Passion in the course of our lives. Even more important—we find them all within ourselves. Judas the betrayer, Peter denying Jesus, Pilate too weak to accept truth, Caiaphas deliberately destroying goodness incarnate, John with faith giving him the courage to be at the Cross, Mary the mother whose love brought her even to Calvary—a time of crisis can reveal where we might have stood at what seemed to be the ultimate disaster of mankind.

3 *The aftermath of disaster*

If Calvary was like a crucifixion of humanity, then one must see in Christ's Resurrection, as Paul recognised, a hope for humanity itself. Evil appeared to be victorious but it was ultimately powerless to destroy the spirit of Jesus. It was that spirit which enabled the Church to survive all attempts to destroy it by forces working inside as well as outside it. There have been times when there seemed to be no reasonable hope of its continuation because of its weakness or corruption. Yet it has outlasted a succession of empires which in their time appeared to be secure and impregnable. This is worth remembering particularly when we are tempted to despair of the Church as it is today, either because of its faults or because of the formidable nature of the forces ranged against it. Nevertheless this does not give us grounds for complacence. Rather should it lead us to admit that the survival of Christianity has depended on the power of God. That power has been conveyed through men and women of integrity and faith who have refused to succumb to disaster, despair or doubt. It is they who have been the instruments through which Christ has fulfilled his promise that the Spirit would guide the Church into all truth. Their response to the dangerous situation has, however, not been any attempt to wrap the Church round in spiritual cellophane, to preserve it exactly as it was in the past. They were well aware that the Church is not an end in itself. Instead, they challenged and helped it to a renewal of its vision even if that meant a painful and penitent re-assessment of priorities. For they were prepared to believe that

God could be speaking to the Church from and through the danger and the disaster.

4 *The road ahead*

This is a lesson from twenty centuries of Christianity which we have to accept for ourselves. It may be that the Church is being called to be a 'pilgrim Church' and to 'travel light' with less material baggage to carry. Possibly it has to think less about itself as a kind of Rock of Ages offering refuge for those who cannot cope with the stresses of the rat-race. Perhaps the Church has to be less bothered about its image, its social involvement, its political witness—and instead, more concerned to consecrate to God whatever is of good in the secular world, but equally concerned to challenge to the point of costly contradiction the values of that world when they are manifestly unsound.

In an age of increasingly rapid change we cannot know what lies ahead either for the world or for the Church. All we can be sure of is that the Church will be called, sent and strengthened for any work that God lays upon it. Christians will have to go where the need is greatest, not where the prospects look best. They will know that Christ is there already, both where there is crucifixion and where there is resurrection.

HOLY WEEK

Maundy Thursday

The trouble with Christianity, for some people, is that it is too 'earthy'. They like its theory but not its practice. They value religion as a philosophy or as a means towards self-fulfilment. They appreciate its devotional aspects but dislike its doctrines which they tend to dismiss as 'dogma'. But they are reluctant to accept a Christianity which asks them to involve themselves in the lives of other people whether in worship, or fellowship or service. Such activities, as well as the use of sacraments, they are inclined to regard as non-essential options pertaining to a kind of materialism irrelevant to spiritual life. Yet we cannot ignore the fact that Christianity is an essentially materialistic religion. It believes that material objects matter in the good purpose of God. It believes that he can work through things and through ordinary human activities. It recognises that human nature being what it is, man needs to see and touch and feel the power of God at work in ways that he can readily comprehend.

This is nowhere more evident than in the methods which our Lord used in teaching his disciples. He employed what we could call visual aids, just as many of the prophets before him had done. He knew that when words and actions and objects were presented together, there was the best possibility of the teaching being remembered.

1 *The night of signs*

This is just what happened on the night before Good Friday. Jesus knew that anxious and fearful as they were, the disciples were in no state to receive teaching which would demand close attention. So instead, he taught them by actions which they would remember. The memory would help to carry them through the trials which lay ahead. When the Twelve had had the meal with him, Jesus took bread, broke it and shared it among them saying 'This is my body'. He blessed the cup of wine and said 'This is my blood of the new covenant'.

He did something more. Taking water and a towel, he washed the feet of each of the disciples. None of them was left out, although for a moment Peter resisted an action which he thought demeaning to his Lord. But Jesus explained that if he as their Master had performed the menial functions of a servant, they must also see themselves as servants of each other. Then when they had sung a psalm of thanksgiving, they went out into the night . . .

This was by no means the first occasion on which Christ gave a spiritual meaning to bread and wine as symbols of his work of redemption. He had asked James and John if they were willing to drink his cup of suffering, when they had thought of the future as one of success and security. He spoke of himself as the bread of eternal life. Another familiar description of himself was that of being the true vine. Wine was one of the tokens of the messianic banquet. It stood for the ferment of the new life, for power and communion.

At the Last Supper it had an added significance. It was linked with the blood of the new covenant being inaugurated with the sacrifice of Christ himself. The purpose of sacrifice was to establish union between the worshipper and his God. At the Supper, Christ said nothing about the worthiness of the recipient. But later Paul, when reminding the Corinthians about the Institution of the Communion, drew from it two significant lessons. One was eschatological. That is to say that the disciples were to re-enact the Communion in remembrance of Jesus until he should return. The other was personal and moral. Paul insisted that there was a serious spiritual risk that men might receive the Body and the Blood 'without discerning'. He did not suggest that only the perfect should communicate. He asked that all should be aware of the spiritual significance of what was happening in the sacrament.

2 The water and the towel

It was the same theological awareness as that for which Jesus had asked in the foot-washing. He knew that the disciples still tended to think of the Kingdom in terms of status and authority. Even at the Ascension in their last conversation with him, their question about the coming of the Kingdom would reflect the same approach. What really mattered was that they should see their role in it as one of humility and service. This was going to be of crucial importance to their witness to the world and their obedience to God. If they had that, then it would be the basis of their own fellowship and of their freedom from material concerns. But their humility would have to be positive and purposeful. Even turning the other cheek and walking the second mile, were not virtues in themselves. These had to be instrumental to their calling and discipleship.

So on that Maundy Thursday night those simple everyday actions conveyed deep truths. They anticipated the crucifixion of the following day, its meaning being incorporated in acts of communion and of mutual service, as they should always be. Our sacred symbols may reflect other aspects of Christ's work and life, as teacher, healer, friend of outcasts, lover of children or carpenter of Nazareth. We regard the empty Cross as the sign of his victory. There was a time, a generation ago, when Christ in Majesty was the most popular of symbols put in churches and the crucifix was looked at askance as somewhat morbid. But it is impossible to know the joy of the Risen Lord without understanding something of the meaning of Good Friday, the climax of a whole life of Atonement. It is the Church, and the Christian, which has experienced the Passion and the Resurrection in its own life that can best meet the needs of mankind. And it will do so with the humility which knows that it has no power of itself—but also can see the powers of the world in their proper perspective.

For in personal life it is humility which enables one to achieve a sense of proportion—and a sense of humour about oneself. It prevents a man taking himself too seriously. It saves him from being caught up in the world's preoccupation with status and reputation, with rights and rewards. He realises how little all these things matter and how little they contribute to the peace of mind and sense of purpose which Christ was sharing with his disciples. So many people today are beginning to realise this and to have suspicions about their own mythology of success. They try to opt out of what they consider to be the 'rat race' but this negative attitude rarely solves their problem. For the 'race' itself is almost inescapable and none of us can walk away from life as we have to live it. What Christ was offering was not a way round our problems, but a way through them. He was not treating them as though they did not exist or did not matter. The writer of the epistle to the Hebrews writes of him, 'We have not a high priest who is unable to sympathise with our weaknesses, but one who in every respect has been tempted as we are, yet without sinning.' This is the incarnation in action. As Paul wrote in Philippians 2.5-7, it began with the supreme act of humility which has to be the example for the ordinary Christian.

So the way of humility is the unique expression of the divine nature in human life as it is of the Godhead in the Manhood in Christ. It is the 'earthing' of faith in action. It has always been an essential part of the Gospel which Christianity has tried to offer to the world. It has been obscured at times when the Church itself has abandoned the way of humility to seek power and glory. It has been gloriously evident in the lives of saints who have asked nothing for themselves save the knowledge that they were serving God and men. And so doing they have recalled the Church to its true vocation, and brought new hope to a world which has seen through its own facade of pomp and circumstance. For they have born witness to the Christ who was born in a stable and died on a cross, possessing nothing but infinite love.

HOLY WEEK

Day of Atonement

Every year on Good Friday, Christendom commemorates with penitence and thanksgiving the supreme sacrifice which our Lord made when he atoned for the sins of mankind and reconciled man to God. He made there in the words of the Prayer Book, 'by his one oblation of himself once offered, a full, perfect, and sufficient sacrifice, oblation, and satisfaction, for the sins of the whole world.' These are tremendous words. What do they mean to us today?

1 *Yom Kippur*

The idea of vicarious sacrifice as an act of atonement would have been more familiar to the Jews of our Lord's time than it is to us today. The most important day in their Kalendar, as it is for Jews of our time, is the Day of Atonement. It occurs on the tenth day of Tishri, the seventh month of the Jewish year, in September-October. A strict fast is demanded and even Jews who may rarely attend worship at other times of the year go to their synagogues. But sacrifices as such are no longer part of Jewish religious practice.

The ritual as it was enacted at the Temple is set out in Leviticus 16 and Numbers 29. Both passages are probably post-exilic but reflect practices of ancient date.

The Day began with the high priest laying aside his customary ornate vestments and putting on simple linen robes. Then he chose two he-goats and cast lots to determine which should be sacrificed and which was to be driven out into the wilderness.

Next, he made atonement for himself and the rest of the priesthood, slaying a bullock and sprinkling its blood in front of the Mercy-Seat and the Ark in the inmost sanctuary. Then he made atonement for the Most Holy Place, the Holy Place and the Outer Court of the Temple, slaying the first goat and sprinkling its blood as he had done earlier.

Finally came the climax of the rite. The high priest made public confession of the sins of the whole nation and, placing his hand on the head of the second goat, transferred the sins to its head. It was then taken out into the wilderness and driven away. In our Lord's time the goat was led to a precipice twelve miles from Jerusalem and hurled over this to its death. The day's proceedings concluded with the high priest resuming his usual vestments and offering burnt-offerings for himself and the people.

The whole ritual expressed the two themes of atonement and reconciliation in this, the supreme act of worship in the Old Testament.

2 Cleansing from sin

Jewish Christians would have had this ritual in mind as they grew to understand the meaning of the Crucifixion. In the epistle which the Church appoints to be read on Good Friday, the writer of Hebrews contrasts the repeated annual sacrifice of the Jewish rite with the self-offering of Jesus, made once for all and effective for ever. 'For by a single offering he has perfected for all time those who are sanctified,' he writes.

The author recognised that the Levitical rite was based upon the concern for holiness and so emphasised the seriousness of sin. To be worthy of God, the priesthood, the sanctuary and the people had to be cleansed. By actions expressing humility, penitence and propitiation the right relation with the deity could be restored. The blood of sacrifice was the dynamic means whereby purification could be accomplished and atonement made for sin. There had to be a complete break with the contagion lingering from the past, even to the extent of cleansing the sacred vestments.

The transfer of the people's sin to the head of the unfortunate scape-goat (literally, the goat that was allowed to escape) may seem strange to us. Behind it lay the idea that sin was almost like a material contagion. They were not transferring their guilt for their sins, in the way the modern use of the term scapegoat signifies someone who carries the blame for another's mistakes. They were all to aware of their own culpability. But the ritual obscured the fact that what could not be transferred was the root cause of sin within man's own heart.

This had to be dealt with from two directions. From the human side, it needed sincere and penetrating repentance. For this, ritual sacrifice was no substitute, according to such prophets as Isaiah and Hosea. From the divine side, only God's direct action could bring the cleansing grace to bear on human nature and deal with it from inside.

3 From atonement to at-one-ment

Thus the Day of Atonement had an additional significance in its preparation for men's minds for the work of Christ, through its continuing emphasis on the fact of sin and the need for repentance. But its message was fulfilled only when the Divine entered human life in the incarnation of Christ.

Our Lord himself taught that sacrifices were no substitute for repentance. He told his disciples that he would give his own life as 'a ransom for many' and so would establish a new covenant. The writer of the Fourth Gospel saw Jesus as the Lamb of God who could take away the sin of the world and as the Lamb sacrificed at the Passover.

But it was, characteristically, the Apostle Paul who fully related the Old Atonement to the New. He saw the death and resurrection of Jesus as means by which man is redeemed from sin, from condemnation and from death. By his self-sacrifice, Jesus had made peace between man and God. In baptism, the Christian mystically shared in the death and in the victory of Jesus. But the New Testament recognises that the whole life of Christ, from the Birth to the Resurrection, was an atonement by the One who redeemed humanity from within. And it was the battle for this truth that lay behind the theological controversies of the next three centuries.

4 *The way of hope*

All this may seem heavily theological for our devotion on Good Friday. But it is called Good because in Old English the word meant 'holy'. And this is the day when we have to contemplate, as they did among the ancient Jews, the mystery of holiness both in respect of the purpose of God and of our calling as Christians. In our devotion we may reflect with sadness on the evil intent of those who put Jesus to death and the weakness of those who deserted him. But we must also think of the present significance of what happened on Calvary. For by his death, Jesus did something of permanent value and relevance, giving men the liberty to live as the children of God. They have to make this potential into actual reality by making the response of faith, in repentance and hope and love, living in the new dimension of people reconciled to God and to each other.

This is the Gospel which has to be taken to heart within the Church before it can be presented effectively to the world. The Day of Atonement ritual rightly began with the cleansing of the priesthood and the sanctuary. At his last meal with the disciples on Maundy Thursday, Jesus gave the cup to his disciples with the words: 'This is my blood of the new covenant, which is shed for you and for many, for the remission of sins.' The 'you' came before the 'many'. For Jesus was concerned, as the Levitical code had been, that the Church should be cleansed so that it might be fit to be used as the instrument of God's purpose in the redemption of the world.

So as we meditate before the Cross on Good Friday, our penitence has to begin with the way in which we fulfil our priesthood, offer our worship, say our prayers, and enter into mutual commitment and love within one Body of Christ. We have to resist the temptation to transfer the blame for our defects to any scape-goat, ancient or modern. We have to let the grace of God into the very heart of our life as a Church and as Christians. We will pray: 'Lord convert thy world and thy Church, beginning with me.'

EASTER

The plural of grief

Some kinds of optimism are illogical luxuries. One is the common assumption that whatever misfortune or disaster may happen to others it will not fall upon oneself. We take this attitude even to the one inescapable and universal experience— death. This is the one certain journey for which few of us prepare. When it occurs to other people, we may behave as though it was an embarrassment. We expect the bereaved to conceal their grief and tears. We hope that they will get over their loss as quickly as possible. Yet it is they who have to come to terms with the loss, not us. They have to learn to live with their situation.

Yet long before we ourselves experience bereavement through the death of someone we love, most of us have to go through many experiences which cause us loss of one kind or another. And the way in which we cope with these, helps us to adjust ourselves to the major bereavement when and if it occurs.

1 *Who are the losers?*

Modern life is a mixture of gains and losses and the balance is continually changing. At one period economic growth is the keynote of the nation. Almost overnight, recession brings widespread redundancy and unemployment.We have to see these changes not as impersonal statistics but in terms of human beings. To most people it is their work that gives their life a great measure of both purpose and status. Its loss is a disaster. Those of us who lived through the depression of the Thirties cannot forget the effects of unemployment on homes and communities. This threat spreads across the whole social spectrum today.

The loss of health is another hazard of contemporary life, to a degree which is surprising when one considers what amazing improvements there have been in medical care in recent decades. Many diseases which were scourges a generation ago have almost disappeared. They have been replaced by stress diseases. Similarly life is endangered by its own speed and complexity of travel and transport.

Apart from the danger of loss of work or health, an increasing proportion of the population is liable to suffer the breakdown of a relationship. The adult or child who is the casualty of a broken marriage, the youngster who has drifted away from home, the old person abandoned by relatives—these are only a few of the 'grief-bearers' of today. Their reaction to the situation may at first be one of numbness or panic. Their sense of isolation may pass off after a while or it may turn into withdrawal from all contacts with others. Society itself may be unhelpful and indifferent. It tends to go on the defensive and to give the impression of resenting its casualties. It expects people to cope with their own problems and if they are unable to do so, then the community assumes that sufficient help is available from official sources. But this can touch only the fringe of what has become an ever-increasing problem of the 'loser' in the community.

2 What can we do?

One has to ask if the Church community might be some value to the outside world in this problem. Its own members include many who go through these situations of loss, and of grief in the broad sense. From the loss of employment, of health, of security in marriage or family life to the agony of bereavement —we are all vulnerable to these disasters. Does our membership of the Church make any difference to us when they occur?

Paul was quite clear that it should do so. He wrote in I Corinthians 12.26: 'If one member suffers, all suffer together. If one is honoured, all rejoice together.' When this actually happens, it reveals a Church which is truly being the Body of Christ.

In one parish, a family was suddenly bereaved by the tragic death of the mother. The local congregation shared responsibility for the five children. In another, two of the congregation were made redundant and their families were in financial straits. Their fellow members helped to find them jobs and supported them in the meantime. But this kind of thing does not always happen. A 'pillar of the Church' fell into a desperate situation and took his own life. This might have been avoided if he had felt able to share his problem with his fellow-Christians. But theirs was the superficial kind of fellowship in which the discussion of personal problems was simply 'not done'. It was the sort of church which is a caricature of the Body of Christ. Its worship was a meeting—and yet not a real meeting—of individuals who never used towards each other the Christian names with which in Baptism they had entered the Church. They hardly every visited each others' homes. They could hardly be said to belong to Christ since they refused to belong to each other in Christ. And if they do not care for each other within their religious fellowship it is highly unlikely that Christians will be able to care for their neighbour outside it.

One of the signs of spiritual progress in the Church today is that such congregations are rare. Many Christians really do translate their caring into action inside and outside the Church. Some do it in their course of their daily work, through voluntary organisations and in their own immediate neighbourhood. They do not wait to be asked. They go out to see where and what the need is. For example, a group of young wives belonging to churches in a northern area are making themselves responsible for providing a creche for the children of wives visiting their husbands in prison. In another district members of the congregation organise the regular visiting of newcomers and house-bound. And whenever one is tempted to take a poor view of human nature, one should remember the vast numbers of members of voluntary societies—including Christians and non-Christians—who are unsparing in giving person-to-person service to people in need. Much of it is done by people who have to face in their own lives the testing times of loss, grief, loneliness and disaster. They know what the situation is like, from inside.

3 The personal situation

The Bible does not evade this problem as it confronts the individual. The Psalmist could write: 'I said in my haste all men are liars.' Psalm 22 begins with the agony of 'My God, my God, why hast thou forsaken me?' It ends with the triumph of faith. But faith has to start with the acceptance of the situation. In 2 Samuel 12, David prayed that his son might be spared. The child died. To the amazement of his courtiers, David did not go through the rituals of mourning. He said 'Now he is dead, why should I fast? Can I bring him back? I shall go to him, but he will not return to me.' He had to take up the threads of life again. But later, when his son Absalom was killed, David had to be reminded that his excessive grief was destroying the morale of the nation. It is not easy for any of us in a situation of loss or bereavement to accept it realistically and to set it in the context of our continuing obligations. Life has to go on and we have to adjust ourselves to new demands in which there may even be new opportunities. Our experience may have taught us something about our priorities. It may also have made us better able to sympathise—the word literally means to 'feel with'—others. This is the renewal which God's grace can bring us. Paul wrote of it in 2 Corinthians 6.10: 'As sorrowful, yet always rejoicing; as poor, yet making many rich; as having nothing, and yet possessing everything.' Loss is real and death is real, but neither is final and we realise this when we face them with the Christ who wept when his friend Lazarus died but who comforted Mary and Martha with the assurance: 'I am the Resurrection and the Life.'

EASTER

Voice from the dead

One of the mysteries of the Gospel is the fact that the Risen Lord revealed himself to so few people. In 1 Corinthians 15, Paul mentions appearances to Peter, to the other disciples, to more than five hundred brethren at once, to James and the rest, and finally to himself 'as to one untimely born'.

Jesus might have been expected to show himself to the multitude or to his enemies. This might have convinced Pilate, Caiaphas and the Sanhedrin of the reality of his resurrection and messiahship. It could have made a vast difference to the history of Christianity and avoided the persecution of the Church in Jerusalem. It might be that Jesus preferred that his Church should take, as he had done, the hard way of faith instead of the easier way of fact.

1 Shock tactics

At the second temptation in the wilderness, Jesus had rejected the possibility of shocking men into belief. He knew that a miraculous descent from the pinnacle of the temple would have an effect which would be immediate but superficial. Men would be temporarily convinced but not lastingly converted.

If they were fundamentally unchanged, neither a miracle nor the sight of him returned from the dead would effect anything.

There is an anticipation of this in the parable about Dives and Lazarus in Luke 16. Here the rich man suffering the torments of hell pleads first for himself. He asks that Abraham will send Lazarus to soothe his agony. When this request is refused, he appeals to Abraham to send Lazarus back to earth to warn his five brothers 'lest they also come into this place of torment'. Abraham replies: 'They have Moses and the prophets; let them hear them.' The rich man argues that if someone goes to them from the dead, they will repent. But Abraham states that if they do not hear Moses and the prophets they would not be convinced even if someone should rise from the dead.

2 The Law says . . .

The point of this parable is clear. The Law and the prophets already provide sufficient guidance in respect of the behaviour which had brought Dives into this situation. His sin was that of total indifference to the needs of his fellow-men. The poor man had lain at the very door of Dives' house, in desperate need of food and healing, while the rich man feasted sumptuously with his friends. The problems of poverty and unemployment might well have been among the topics of conversation at his dinner table. But he had never felt inclined to do anything personally about them.

Dives would have heard the Law and the prophets read and expounded often enough in the synagogue, with their message of obligation to one's neighbour. He might have felt that he was fulfilling this adequately by conventional almsgiving. But this was no substitute for responsible involvement with someone right on his doorstep. This would be equally true of his brothers. The return of Lazarus would have no real effect upon men whose lives were based on essentially wrong principles. So Lazarus could not return to confront the brothers of Dives. Neither did Jesus return to confront his enemies.

3 Witness to the resurrection

Jesus showed himself only to those who loved him and had believed in him. He did so to establish their faith, perhaps also to assure them of forgiveness for having failed him. And he made clear that they, not he himself, were to be the witnesses to the resurrection. The experience transformed their lives. Their experience and their message were to be taken together out into the world. He said: '*You* shall be my witnesses.' They took this seriously. When the time came to appoint an apostle to take the place of the traitor Judas, they were certain they should choose someone who had accompanied them throughout Christ's mission and could also be a witness to his resurrection.

It is significant also that both at Pentecost and when preaching later to the Jews, the apostles took up the theme exemplified in the parable of Dives and Lazarus. They did not simply report the fact of the resurrection. They also reminded their hearers of 'Moses and the Prophets'. They showed that the mission and message of Jesus, even his crucifixion which was anathema to Jewish traditionalists, was the fulfilment of the purpose of God as already revealed in the Old Testament. This was much more than a collection of proof-texts. It put the Risen Lord in the context of the continuing purpose of God throughout Israel's history.

4 The Church of the Resurrection

In the trials which beset the Church, Christians are sometimes tempted to long for the Risen Lord to reveal himself and confront the world. It is not easy to apply to ourselves the message which underlies the words of Abraham in the parable. But we have the evidence already in the Gospel, in the transformed life of the disciples, in the power of the living Christ dwelling in his Body throughout the ages. The real question is not what effect a new resurrection would have, but what part our faith in the resurrection plays in our lives already.

Paul had no illusions about the importance of this question.

In 1 Corinthians 15, he insisted that if Christ had not risen, then Christian preaching is vain and Christian works pointless. This is the heart of Christianity and there is no substitute for it. Then, as now, it was possible for the Church to be a witness to almost everything except the resurrection. Its gospel might be one of gloom and doom, its life one of arid austerity with no semblance of joy and thankfulness. Its attention could be wholly absorbed by the maintenance of its power or by bustling activism. It might see itself as a society for the exclusive salvation of its members. But if any of these were its chief priority, then the Church would cease to be 'the divine society' existing to convey God's grace and to be the instrument of his purpose.

In its creeds the Church affirms its belief in the resurrection. But the proof of its sincerity lies in what it shows in its life. For instance, as a Church we may face contemporary problems which seem insoluble. Our tasks are beyond our resources. We are all too aware of weaknesses within Christendom. Or, alternatively, we make plans and develop policies confident that we know the answers to all our problems. At what point do we bring the Risen Lord into our thinking and action? This is more than just a conventional prayer for guidance. It is really putting into effect what Paul called being 'in Christ'. When Jesus said 'I am with you always', his words were a challenge as well as a comfort. We have to act on this promise in the committee meeting and the act of worship, in the factory and the prayer-group, in the ministry to the broken and in confronting the power-structures of the world.

The apostles knew this same experience in personal life. Paul could write: 'I can do all things through Christ who strengthens me.' That was after a lifetime of solitary exposure to one difficult situation after another. He knew that in every one of them Christ was there already, not simply as an idea or an ideal but as a living presence. And this was the Christ who had been through every human situation himself. For the Risen Lord was the Jesus of Gethsemane and Golgotha as well as Galilee.

This mystical union has perhaps never been better expressed than in the words of St Patrick's Breastplate:

> Christ be with me, Christ within me,
> Christ behind me, Christ before me,
> Christ beside me, Christ to win me,
> Christ to comfort and restore me,
> Christ beneath me, Christ above me,
> Christ in quiet, Christ in danger,
> Christ in hearts of all that love me,
> Christ in mouth of friend and stranger.

EASTER

Breakfast for twelve

The teenagers were talking about family life. One of them remarked: 'The only time we eat together as a family is on Christmas Day!' He may have been exaggerating. But he was touching on one of the changes in domestic life of recent years. With both parents at work and the youngsters pursuing their own interests, many families rarely spend much time together at meals. They also tend to extend hospitality to friends and neighbours less frequently than they used to do.

This seems far removed from family life as it appears in the New Testament. Christians then were 'given to hospitality'. When they came together for worship the common meal was a natural part of fellowship. It would not have seemed remarkable to them that there are so many references to meals in the Gospels. At every one of them something significant occurred. One can think of the wedding feast at Cana, or of the time when Martha protested that Mary was neglecting her share of the household duties. In the last week at Jerusalem it was at a meal that Jesus was anointed by a woman of rare insight. And above all, there was the Last Supper. So it is not surprising that the Fourth Gospel ends its narrative of the Passion and Resurrection with the account of the meal by the lakeside.

1 Feed my sheep

The incident begins when Peter, impatient as ever of inactive waiting, decided to go out fishing. The ten others went with him. They fished through the night and caught nothing. As they brought the boat in towards the shore, they saw someone waiting at the water's edge. He called to them to cast their nets on the other side of the boat and they were immediately successful. The disciple John said that it must be the Lord. Peter slipped over the side of the boat and swam the hundred yards or so to land. There they found that Jesus had prepared a charcoal fire with bread and fish. So they breakfasted together.

After the meal a strange dialogue took place. Jesus, calling Peter by the old name of Simon, asked him if he loved him. This happened three times and each time Peter was told to 'feed my sheep'. Peter was hurt by this questioning of his love. Then Jesus forecast that Peter would indeed prove his love by martyrdom. The Lord's final word to him was that which he had spoken when he first called Peter to discipleship: 'Follow me.' It has been suggested that all this was Christ's reminder to Peter that he had three times denied his master. Be that as it may, at this their last meal together, Jesus was laying upon his disciples the obligation of shepherding his sheep and lambs. As shepherds, they were to continue the work of the Great Shepherd himself.

2 Pastoral responsibility

Jesus was not making a suggestion to his disciples. He was making a specific demand for the fulfilment of an inescapable obligation of apostleship. The analogy of shepherding was no conventional or sentimental description of their ministry. It occurs more frequently in the fourth Gospel than in any of the others and the writer was a realist. Shepherding was a hard and lonely life. The shepherd knew every member of the flock as individuals. He had to be prepared to defend them with his life. If one of them had gone astray, he had to be ready to take risks and leave the rest while he went to rescue the stray. It was his job to find pasturage for them, travelling over many miles of country. And always he went in front of them, just as one sees shepherds doing today in Palestine. So the image of the shepherd was truly applicable to the demands of apostleship, in respect of leadership, foresight, intimate knowledge of the flock and courage in defending them.

It is interesting to follow the ways in which Peter and the other apostles tried to fulfil this responsibility in the early days of the Church. This was to them the flock of Christ of which they were shepherds, not owners. They brought newcomers into the fold and saw that they were sustained in it. When the Church came under attack from the Jewish leaders, they were in the forefront of its defence. But problems arose within the flock itself. One was the petty bickering between the foreign and the native-born Jewish Christians over the rations for widows. On this matter Peter took a step which was to have far-reaching consequences. He insisted that the oversight exercised by the apostles had to be directed to more important functions than merely 'serving tables'. So authority over this matter was delegated to seven 'deacons'. But these too, and of them especially Stephen, were caught up in a new departure in shepherding—the witness to the outside world.

This led to the persecution of the Church in Jerusalem. It was driven out into Judea and Samaria, to the old Philistine cities of the coastal strip, up into Syria and across to Cyprus. The Holy Spirit was manifestly confirming the rightness of this new enterprise. But it needed the vision of Paul to embody in a revolutionary policy the full pastoral mandate of Jesus. For he had said, again according to John's record, 'Other sheep have I which are not of this fold.' This was, to Paul, the mystery of God's purpose now revealed in Christ. For the mission of the Church was not so much an outreach from those within the fold to those outside it. It was a proclamation to those who did not know it, that they belonged to God.

3 Two flocks

The dual pastoral responsibility, towards the flock within the fold and to those outside it, is a continuing commitment of the

Church. Paul charged his congregations to minister to each other's needs, physical, moral or spiritual. Many of his letters end with detailed instructions about this. The Christians are to 'bear one another's burdens and so fulfil the law of Christ'. This passage in Galatians 6 refers particularly to helping those who have fallen under temptation. He would not have accepted the notion that a Christian can maintain such a barrier between his membership of the Church and his private life that he would not think of sharing any personal difficulties with the fellow-members in Christ, not even with those ordained to exercise pastoral responsibility. The pastoral and the priestly ministry is a means whereby the grace of God is brought to bear on the problems of daily life from which not one of us is free. We are Christ's flock in need of his shepherding—even if it takes a certain amount of humility to recognise that at times our behaviour is all too similar to that of sheep!

When a Church experiences in itself this mutual support and active caring, then it is the better able to offer a pastoral ministry to the flock of Christ which is the whole world. Going back to the analogy of the shepherd, we remember that this meant his having a real knowledge of the flock. So we have to ask ourselves what depth of understanding the Church has of the world it may be trying to help. It might be engaged in meeting needs which no longer exist and then it wonders why its help is rejected as irrelevant. The competent shepherd knows the flock and the territory in which it is pasturing. A congregation has to be sensitive to the social problems and developments, the political and industrial changes and the like, of its context. For these are what bear upon the lives of the people it would seek to help. There is little value in a Church which encapsulates itself from its human environment.

But shepherding meant leadership. 'Giving a lead' is not just a responsibility of ecclesiastical dignitaries, nor is it confined to moral questions of the day. It is shared throughout the whole Church, to be exercised in deed as well as in word. It is a leadership in the pilgrimage of truth, challenging false values and constructively criticising plans and policies. But it is also a leadership in the ministry of compassion which seeks out the despairing and the lonely and the broken—as well as those who are lost but do not know it.

For the final charge to Peter was a charge to every Christian, to care for Christ's flock, which is all mankind.

WHITSUNTIDE

Christian boldness

It is difficult for us to appreciate how shocked the Jewish and Gentile world was by the apparently outrageous claims of Christianity. It was bad enough to see Jesus consorting with social outcasts, breaking the Sabbath, criticising the traditions which had grown up around the Law, and paying scant respect to the religious Establishment. It was intolerable when his followers eventually moved out into the world and accepted converts from paganism.

Even then the Gospel was regarded with suspicion. The claim of Christians to regard God as their Father and the Son of God as their brother, seemed to the Greeks to reflect exactly the 'hubris' or excessive pride which their mythology treated as most offensive to the gods. What made matters worse was that so many of these Christians were slaves or from the lowest ranks of society. Bernard Shaw makes this point very clearly in the play *Androcles and the Lion*. The hero is a 'smelly little tailor' despised by the patrician centurion. Similarly in Shaw's *Major Barbara* the aristocratic heroine of the twentieth century has the audacity to treat people out of the gutter as her brothers and sisters in Christ.

1 *The boldness of the church*

Faced with this kind of opposition and criticism, the early Christians sometimes lost their nerve. The Jewish Church in Jerusalem was uneasy about the hostility of their fellow Jews.

They besought Paul to do something which would allay suspicions by demonstrating his loyalty to the Law. So doing, they started the process which led to his arrest and eventually to his death.

Outside Palestine it could be equally difficult for them to remain steadfast. Paul had constantly to encourage his converts not to be dismayed by their lowly social status. In 1 Corinthians 1.26-29 he acknowledged that few of them were wise, powerful or of noble birth. But they had to remember that God had deliberately chosen them and the source of their new status was Christ. On the other hand, in other parts of the New Testament, the converts had to be warned not to give offence to the outside world but to bear reproach and misrepresentation with meekness. This was a very real dilemma for the Christians. It could mean costly decisions in questions of principle and practice when they had to face persecution and even martyrdom. But when confronted by 'tribulation, distress, persecution, famine, nakedness, peril or sword' they remembered that 'If God is for us, who can be against us?' They believed that nothing could 'separate us from the love of God in Christ Jesus our Lord'. Without their boldness, the Church would have ceased to exist.

2 The power of faith

In some ways it is more difficult to witness with boldness in the modern world than it was in New Testament times. The first Christians had themselves experienced the visible presence of Christ or would know others who had done so. Many of them believed that the End was near and their Lord's return imminent. They took the evidence of the gifts of the Spirit as confirming the rightness of their cause and calling. They were also convinced that Christ had put an end to the power of the old religions.

Rightly or wrongly, contemporary Christianity is much less self-confident. It feels some measure of guilt in respect of its own past in such matters as resistance to social reform, opposition to scientific progress and tolerance of religious divisiveness.

It is uncertain about its role in a rapidly changing society. It is worried about its decline in membership and resources, and confused by the pressure of secularism and permissiveness in the climate of opinion. The resurgence of the great ethnic religions such as Hinduism, Buddhism and Islam has made Christendom more ready to understand the significance and value of those religions. But it has also made Christianity less willing to understand and present the revelation of God in Christ as unique and all-embracing. The Fourth Gospel reports Jesus as having said plainly 'No one comes to the Father but by me'. In his epistle to the Colossians, Paul affirmed the total adequacy of Jesus in whom 'all the fulness of God was pleased to dwell, and through him to reconcile to himself all things . . . ' It was this complete faith in the divinity of Christ which was the ground of the boldness of the early Christians. Upon the recovery of this faith depends the renewal of Christian confidence in the present generation.

It was not a cynic but a true man of God who remarked recently that the trouble with modern theology is that so few theologians appear to believe in God! We have plenty of theologies of different kinds such as a theology of work, or money, of art, of social service etc. But theology is essentially the study of God himself, not of theories about him and in the light of this we recognise that the whole of life is 'theological'. At every Sunday service we state our justification for being there at all when we say: 'I believe in God.' If this is a statement of fact, then all else has meaning. If we do not believe, then our worship is merely a social exercise, our evangelism is little more than a membership-recruitment campaign, and our 'Gospel' becomes a mixture of good advice and negative denunciation of the naughty world.

3 The ground of boldness

The interesting thing about the 'boldness' of these Christians of the first century is that the word meant literally 'free speech'. Confidently and without fear, they spoke to God and to men. Their approach to God was the basis of their approach to the world. They were well aware of their own faults and short-comings. But they were certain of the divine forgiveness conveyed to them by Christ. They believed that the Holy Spirit would not desert them but would cleanse and guide them. There were many times when they might have despaired of themselves, let alone of the tasks which confronted them. But they went back to God in penitence, thanking him for every sign of growth, thanking him for their vocation even when it entailed suffering and sacrifice. These were very ordinary people faced with as many difficulties as we encounter today—in many ways probably greater than we have. But they had a profound sense of dependence on God and brought him into every decision which they had to make.

This gave them a sense of instrumentality. They believed themselves to be Christ's agents in the redemption and recon-ciliation of the world. They saw the Church as Christ's inven-tion and Christ's intention, a divine society and not a man-made organisation for the promotion of good causes. This was the source of their authority and of the vocation which they had to live up to.

The other element in their boldness was their sense of being what Paul described as 'in Christ' and doing things together with him. One of the striking features of Paul's vocabulary is the very large number of verbs to which he adds the word 'with'. Christians are, for example, 'buried-with' Christ in baptism, 'crucified-with' him in mystical death, 'raised-with' him in the resurrection. And it is with Christ that Christians worship, in his real presence. It is with Christ that the Christian Church comes to life and goes into every new situation to which it is called by the voice of God and the needs of the world. In Christ it bears the four marks of being One, Holy, Catholic and Apostolic. One in a God-given unity, Holy with the holiness which is the gift of the Spirit, Catholic in its concern to know and proclaim the whole truth, and Apostolic in being sent with its commission: 'Go, make disciples, baptise and teach . . . ' the whole Gospel with boldness and freedom.

Take your gift away

Imagine two women in church on a Sunday morning in Philippi. At the Eucharist, instead of a sermon, there is being read a letter from their beloved friend and founder, Paul, who is far away in prison. He thanks God as he remembers the Philippians and goes on to give them inspiring counsel. Then suddenly there is a change of mood:

'I beseech Euodia and I beseech Syntyche to agree in the Lord.'

Paul has heard about the disagreement between these two 'pillars of the church'. It is not only affecting their relationship. It is also dividing the Church. The two women were probably too shocked and embarrassed to take in the glorious words with which the apostle concludes.

This was not the only occasion on which the Apostle had to rebuke members of a congregation. He had to challenge the Corinthians for turning the Agape into a display of one-upmanship, like a competition in lunch-baskets. Forgetting the spiritual nature of the Bread and the Cup at the Communion, they had committed something akin to sacrilege. Elsewhere he did not hesitate to single out individuals or groups who were destroying the unity of the Body. This was not a new scrupulosity peculiar to Paul. He was only continuing Christ's own emphasis on the personal and moral implications of participating in worship.

1 *At the point of worship*

This is exemplified in a passage in the Sermon on the Mount. Jesus was telling his disciples that their righteousness must exceed that of the Scribes and Pharisees. This must have seemed to be a rather unrealistic demand, for these leaders were outstanding in their keeping of the Law. Moreover it appeared to contradict Christ's own practice for the general impression was that he did not take too seriously the many regulations and restrictions which surrounded the observance of the Law.

But Jesus explained that he was asking for an inward righteousness which lay far deeper than ritual observance. For example, when a man came to bring his gift to the altar and there remembered that he was at odds with his brother, he must leave his gift there without offering it. He must return immediately and be reconciled to his brother. Only then could he come and make his offering. This was a matter of urgency, for at any moment he might have to face the judgement.

Our Lord was giving a new content to the meaning of righteousness. It had been thought of in terms of legal correctness in obedience to the will of God conveyed and expressed in the Law. The breach of this would be judged and punished. Prophets like Amos had humanised this concept, teaching that God's righteousness included a special concern for the poor and helpless and so required benevolence and kindness in the treatment of the needy. The idea of conformity to the divine will is restated in the teaching of Jesus. But the will of God is broadened to relate to right behaviour towards one's fellowmen and to one's attitude towards them. In this passage it is implied that when man is engaged in his highest religious activity of the worship of God, then his right dealing towards others is not something outside the sphere of worship. It is very relevant to it. Up to a point we acknowledge this when, during corporate worship, we use words of general confession about our sins of thought and word and deed against our neighbours. But the words of Jesus go far beyond this. He asks for immediate action in making redress. He is saying that we dare not come to worship until we have made an act of reconciliation.

2 A new demand

This was indeed a new aspect of righteousness to put before his Jewish hearers. It must have seemed even more revolutionary when presented to Gentile converts. In religion as they had previously known it, worship had little if any relation to conduct. One propitiated the gods, offered sacrifices and went through rituals intended to bring security or prosperity. Even religious prostitution was regarded as normal in some sanctuaries. The secret rituals of the mysteries were designed to offer a kind of deliverance from the prison of the body and material elements, sometimes with a promise of security beyond death. If the Romans and Greeks looked for moral guidance, they turned less to gods and temples than to philosophers.

So Gentile Christians would have difficulty in understanding a theological ethic, a code of conduct based upon belief in God. Even harder would it have been for them to appreciate that religion asked questions about motives and inner dispositions towards other people. They had to be converted to Christianity as to an all-embracing way of life and of thought.

3 A question of discipline

The apostles did not hesitate to put this standard of righteousness before the Church and to ask for a high level of discipline. This theme runs through many of the New Testament letters. They believed it to be necessary for the Church itself if it was to be truly the Body of Christ. It was also essential if the Church was to witness and evangelise. It was not a negative puritanism but a positive holiness, which they inculcated.

Seeing themselves with this vocation and sustained by God's grace, they could not compromise with the permissive society of their age. The temptation to do so has recurred throughout the centuries and it has taken different forms. It has been strongest when the Church was weak and confused, or when it was obsessed with power and status. It is with us today. Yet we have to recognise that in its own moral uncertainty, the world somehow expects the Church to demonstrate the righteousness which is both holy and compassionate. That is true however perversely the world seems to enjoy criticising the Church and to rejoice over its occasional scandals. It seems to be aware that a Church which has no standards, stands for nothing.

So righteousness may involve positive challenge on moral issues of purity, respect for human values, justice for the oppressed and under-privileged, political or administrative corruption and the like. But we have to remember what our Lord said about those who would judge others, however well-intentioned their motives. In the analogy of the mote and the beam, he put a firm challenge not only to the religious leaders of his time but also to the Church of every age. The Epistle to Diognetus, written in the second century, contains the statement that as the soul is to the body, so is the Church to the world. If that high vocation is to be fulfilled, then it requires a standard of righteousness, in the meaning which Jesus gave to it, accepted by every member of the body of Christ.

4 *The personal test*

Jesus applied it to the man who came to worship with hate in his heart. Paul put the quarrel between two Christian women in the same context.

In one congregation there were two cousins. They had not spoken to each other for twenty years because of an ancient quarrel over a will. They came to church every Sunday, sitting as far apart as possible. They regularly made their communion at the same service. Their parish priest prepared his young people for confirmation and taught them their Christian duties. But he knew the youngsters would have constantly before their eyes two people whose way of life denied the Christian Gospel which he was trying to teach. All attempts to heal the breach had failed and, in fact, had been strongly resented. Perhaps Paul would have had the courage to call the congregation to 'discipline' these two people. The Prayer Book rubric required that anyone who is 'an open and notorious liver, or has done any wrong to his neighbours by word and deed . . . shall be advertised that he presume not to come to the Lord's Table . . . ' etc.

The Church took that seriously in 1662. What would happen if we dared to act on it today? We may think we are less 'puritanical', more broadminded and more tolerant towards sins inside the Church as well as outside it. Yet this may be because we have lost sight of the relation between the moral character of the Church and its witness to the world. This is not advocating a 'holier than thou' attitude. Instead it is a call to holiness for the world's sake. And it is a positive and joyous holiness. Paul saw it as based on truth and love, forgiveness and humility, in obedience to the command of Christ:

'Let your light so shine before men, that they may see your good works and give glory to your Father which is in heaven.'

WHITSUNTIDE

Ask the right question

'O peoples, nations and languages, when you hear the sound of the horn, pipe, lyre, trigon, harp, bagpipe, and every kind of music, you are to fall down and worship the golden image that King Nebuchadnezzar has set up; and whoever does not fall down and worship shall immediately be cast into a burning fiery furnace.'

This text from Daniel 3.4 conjures up an engaging picture of the national orchestra of Babylon at the ready. The other kinds of music would have included flutes, pipes and trumpets, with tambourines and castanets for the percussion. All would probably have been played in unison, for harmony as such was unknown. Music was widely employed in worship and there it may well have begun. Its purpose was both to affect the emotions of the worshippers and to bring about results on the godward side. It was not intended for pleasure, but to achieve results.

The results intended in this particular instance was very clear. The music was a signal for the worship of the king as god. This fact was recognised by the three Jewish exiles who had risen to high positions in Babylon. Shadrach, Meshach and Abednego refused to bow down before the image even if it meant death, for this would be contrary to their religious beliefs. With superb courage they declared that they were not prepared to conform to the royal decree even if God did not deliver them. They did not expect him to perform a miracle on their behalf. They accepted life or death, as he willed.

The story has a happy ending. The three men were thrown into the furnace. They walked in it unscathed, accompanied by a mysterious fourth person whose appearance was 'like a son of the gods'.

1 What does it mean?

The value of this story does not depend on whether or not it is historically accurate. Its significance lies in what it says about a question which has to be asked in many different situations. The three heroes of this tale dared to ask 'What does it really mean?' about an apparently unimportant act of conformity. Six hundred years later, Christians did the same when urged to sprinkle incense on the imperial censers in the amphitheatre—a seemingly insignificant gesture of courtesy to the emperor. They believed that to do this would imply that they were accepting the divinity of Caesar and denying Christ. So they refused. Their martyrdom stirred men and women to ask similarly fundamental questions about their own lives—and to ask about life itself the question 'What does it mean?'

2 Take nothing for granted

Their example may be appreciated in this modern age. For ours is a generation when people ask radical questions about many things which our predecessors took for granted such as the monarchy, Parliament, democracy, education, capital, labour, progress, welfare . . . there are no limits. The young particularly are less interested in the history, status or authority of any traditional institution, than in demanding to know what is the use of it.

Even the formerly sacred idol of science is examined critically. Its developments have made immense differences to many realms of life, but not all of them have been beneficial. There is considerable unease about the social and ecological consequences of certain lines of research. It is sometimes argued that science is justified in its own right and that it is the responsibility of society to decide what should be done with its products. Yet in all honesty one must admit that society as a whole, including its governments, is rarely able to understand what is being done and what are its implications. Society is not governed by infallible or omnicompetent beings but by men and women like other folk. Their decisions can be influenced by vested interests concerned with power or profit, with an eye to immediate advantages rather than long-term consequences. So it is important that the decision-makers in every region of a nation's life should know that they have to face the constructive questioning of those who want to know about any plan or policy, what it means and what is the use of it, for the future as well as for the present time.

3 Questioning the Church

We expect radical questions to be put to our institutions without their being resented. The same must be true of the Church. It must be recognised that the question 'What is the use of the Church?' starts from a very different premise from that of the past. Those who ask it now do so in an increasingly secular society in whose education religion plays a rapidly decreasing role. Furthermore, the question could have once been answered by showing the Church's direct contribution to the community in education, and in the care of the young and the sick. In the middle ages the Church also provided an educated civil service. During the last century, its missions have pioneered medical, educational and literacy work and agricultural development.

Most of those functions are now taken over by the state. In some countries there is a movement towards restricting the Church's freedom to give direct service to the community through the traditional avenues. It is told that its task is 'spiritual' and therefore it has no right to do or say anything that has political, social, economic or racial implications. But the Church believes that the whole life of man is God's concern, so the Church must be involved in it. It has to be there in the world, asking the right questions and helping to find the right answers. In John's phrase, it must be seen to be 'doing the truth'. This is a 'use' of the Church which can be understood and valued by a generation which is confused and deafened by the clamour of propaganda and the hard sell of ideologies.

In its pastoral ministry, Christianity at its best is once again trying to meet the needs of men and women as they are now and where they are now. In this it allies itself with many outside its membership who are equally concerned about the problems of humanity. For the Church has no monopoly of concern or of readiness to give service. And another of its contributions has to be that of helping people to become part of a caring community and to accept responsibility for each other.

But no less important is the 'use' of the Church as the Body of Christ which prays for the world as it demonstrates the reality of God's grace. If it is itself reconciled to God, it has to offer a way of reconciliation to the world. This is at the heart of the priestly function of Christendom.

4 *The question is personal*

Stephen Spender once wrote: 'Modern man no longer asks if Christianity is true. He asks what it means.' But how, and whom, does he ask? He may put the question in argument and discussion. But on the whole he tends to do so silently as he evaluates the lives of Christians with whom he is in contact. For he is looking to see what meaning their religion has given them in terms, for instance, of their integrity, their behaviour under stress or suffering, their relationships or even their sense of humour. He is, after all, only applying to them Christ's prophetic word: 'By their fruits you shall know them.'

The fruits of what? Paul saw them as the fruits of the Spirit. Love, joy, peace, patience, kindness, goodness, faithfulness, gentleness, and self-control were not external characteristics with which men clothed themselves by their own efforts. They were the outward and visible signs of the presence of inward and spiritual grace—in fact, a kind of sacrament in reverse.

It is by this criterion that we too shall know ourselves and know the depth of our faith, the reality of our prayer, the width of our love and the measure of fellowship with Christ.

For it is Christ who gives meaning to the Christian and to the Church and to the world.

WHITSUNTIDE

They used helps

The Eastern Mediterranean in winter can be dangerous. No one knew this better than the man who was fairly certain that he was making his last journey across it. This was Paul, on his way to stand trial in Rome. Instead of wintering in a safe harbour, the shipmaster had decided to press on. They ran into trouble from a north-easterly gale which continued for a fortnight, driving them westwards. The ship was taking a hammering from wind and waves. The consequent strain would be very great on a vessel with one large mast midships. So it was decided to 'use helps undergirding the ship'. This meant passing cables under the hull and tightly securing them on the deck, rather like tying a parcel. This process was used right up to the early nineteenth century. Sailors call it 'frapping'.

It worked for a while, but morale began to get low. Then Paul took charge. He said he was certain that all the crew and passengers would be saved. But he insisted that they ate some food. So all 276 on board had a meal. Paul turned it into something more. He 'said grace' and made it a kind of Communion for all these folk in desperate peril. It became a spiritual help which undergirded the ship in a very different sense. When eventually the ship ran aground on the coast of Malta and broke up, everyone on board was saved.

1 A time of crisis

Paul knew that in a time of crisis morale was all important. This is so at any time of danger and particularly in war. One of the objects of training and discipline is that of overcoming the panic which fear can cause. Another important element is the sense of mutual dependence, with the knowledge that one can rely upon the others in the group, as they are relying upon one's own effort. But even more significant for morale can be the power of a common purpose, of greater moment than the immediate issue of facing a common danger or enemy. This may be the deep conviction that one is defending a fundamental principle and value. At such times, a man can be inspired to rise above the ordinary level of endeavour and to achieve his 'finest hour'. The tragedy is that so frequently when the crisis is past the unity disappears, the values fade and self-interest becomes once more the dominant motive. That is one reason why there is no end to wars. In the apathy which succeeds one struggle, the seeds of the next are sown. Men fail to recognise that peace can be a time of crisis no less than can war. To maintain it, men need to 'use helps'.

2 A question of morale

It was the genius of Paul to recognise that the real nature of the crisis was one of morale. At the present time we have no lack of experts offering their analyses of current problems, their origin and their solution. This is the age of global introspection. But very few of their inquiries seem to penetrate to the depths of the malaise of humanity which would appear to be a problem of morale. This the dictionary defines as 'moral condition, especially in respect of confidence and discipline'.

It is not unreasonable to ask what confidence man puts in his leaders and governments, in his neighbours and even in himself. As to the first of these, there seems to have developed a vast gulf between the governors and the governed, which makes men cynical about government and democratic institutions. Then they become vulnerable to totalitarian exploitation, as has happened already.

The neighbour, in the mass society, can become an anonymous threat to one's security. The family weakens under pressure. It ceases to be based on mutual faithfulness and the casualties are the broken lives of parents and children. And as to confidence in oneself, it may be noted that over half the hospital beds in the developed countries may be taken up by cases of mental illness. It is also significant that some of the most sophisticated nations have the highest suicide rates.

As for the other side of morale, where confidence is weak it is impossible to expect discipline in the true sense. This is not the discipline which is imposed from without by increasing rules and restrictions. It is that which proceeds from within, the willing discipline of the self for a common purpose.

3 The Christian in crisis

In such a situation Paul identified himself with his fellow-passengers. He was not concerned to save himself, with an 'I'm all right, Jack' attitude. Because he cared about others he was ready to share with them his own spiritual resources. Sometimes Christians try too hard to be 'in the world but not of the world'. We are of the world, whether we like it or not. Christ's Incarnation happed for the sake of the world, not merely for the sake of the godly. So we have to ask ourselves what our own morale is like, what degree of confidence and discipline we demonstrate and what are the 'helps' which undergird the ship of our lives, as Christians. Now Paul was a very practical and realistic saint. In an emergency he did not indulge in generalities and high-sounding speeches. Neither must we when we set out what in our experience gives us most strength and unity.

One obvious factor is the quality of corporate fellowship which a Church achieves. Peter in prison could count on the prayers of his fellow Christians. Christians in separate cells in a twentieth-century concentration camp sustained each other with shouts of 'Christ is risen' early on Easter morning. In the face of terrorism and oppression, groups of Christians have stayed together and even grown in numbers as the living Body of Christ. They have been able to counter the strategy of the enemy which is always one of 'divide and conquer'. This is not a mere togetherness of superficial fair-weather fellowship. It is a profound sense of belonging to each other in Christ. It sustains the individual member in a personal emergency. It can also offer some example and help to a divided world trying to find a pattern of community for itself.

4 *Sacramental renewal*

The corporate life of the Church itself has to be sustained not only by its own efforts but even more by the grace of God. And this is the meaning and purpose of the Sacraments. Each of the sacraments of Baptism and Holy Communion, Confirmation, Ordination, Matrimony, Absolution and Unction has a personal significance, conveying as it does the grace of God to the individual recipient. But it has also a corporate significance which has sometimes been neglected. It is good that the custom of a kind of 'private' baptism in church is giving way to a truly public baptism in the presence of the congregation. In the sacrament of penance the penitent is restored to the Church which he has wounded by his sin. It would have some advantage if the Church were more adequately represented when a marriage is solemnised. But it is significant that recent revisions of the service of Holy Communion have re-emphasised that this is worship by the whole people of God in one place.

The grace of God is made available to all as well as to the individual. But whether corporate or individual in its operation, the power is that of God not of man. Its efficacy does not depend on the worthiness of the group or of any single recipient. And when either is going through an inner crisis of faith or weakness, that grace is still there to be received. This is the way God works, conveying spiritual force in material forms. The principle of the Incarnation operates in every sacrament.

It may be that the renewal of the Church needs as much as anything else to be a sacramental renewal. We may have forgotten this when we have been so busy renewing our structures and our liturgies, re-assessing our sociological and political priorities, developing ecumenical relationships and working out new forms of ministry. All these are important and yet over-concentration upon them reminds one uncomfortably of the way in which they tried to save the ship on

Paul's fateful journey, by jettisoning cargo and rearranging the equipment!

Paul saved the ship by strengthening morale, meeting the very real physical needs, and sharing with the others his faith in the power of God. One man did for the rest of the 276 what they could not do for themselves, and he did it by the help of God. This is the help that matters most.

WHITSUNTIDE

The Christian steward

It has been said that every man is a capitalist at heart, whatever may be his politics. There is some truth in that if it implies that each of us needs to have something which is his own to express and fulfil himself thereby. But men's ideas as to what is theirs, vary considerably. For some, possession includes 'my job, my money, my house, my rights or my vote'. Others apply ownership in some degree of people too—'my wife, my children or my friends.' And most of us think of existence itself as the ultimate possession for it is 'my life' to do what I will with.

All this seems simply human nature. But Jesus looked at ownership from a completely different angle. In the life of the Kingdom as he described it, what mattered most was not possession but stewardship. In other words, whatever a man had was on loan from his heavenly Father. He had entrusted it to them to enable them to fulfil their vocation as his children. And they would be accountable to him for their us of it. This included even the grace and forgiveness. One of Christ's most powerful parables was about a steward who was forgiven an enormous debt by his master, but went out immediately and demanded payment of a trifling sum by a fellow-servant. Life itself was also on loan. The man who sought to keep it to serve only his self-interest, would lose what he tried to preserve. He could be called to account for it at any time, when he least expected to have to do so.

But God did not expect men to accomplish the impossible by their own efforts. As Paul testified, the grace of God was sufficient for men to make the best use of whatever he entrusted to them. The Father gave men power according to their tasks, not tasks according to their power. Yet, as implied in the parable of the talents, the Father expects men to take risks, confident of his support and his fairness. They are to share what they have, not keep it to themselves. This was Paul's parting message to the Ephesians and he quoted a saying of our Lord's which does not actually appear in the Gospels: 'It is more blessed to give than to receive.' For stewardship means sharing, as well as accountability.

1 *Stewardship today*

Nowadays in church life stewardship is a term used mainly about the giving of money. But this is not a reduction to a materialistic level of the high principle enunciated by our Lord. We may talk largely about such aspects of church membership as witness, service or evangelism. But an acid test of our commitment very often lies in what we do with our money. We have to look at the way in which our expenditure reflects our priorities. Every one has his personal scale of these. It is shown in the amounts he spends on the necessities of daily living for himself and his family. Here it is worth remembering that the luxuries of one generation become the necessities of the next. The amount one spends on what one regards as essential or on the extras, depends on a variety of factors. They include one's habits and interests and one's ideas as to status. One is also influenced by the priorities of the group and class to which one belongs.

An important question, particularly for the Christian, is the extent to which one's religion influences decisions in this matter. At the deepest level, Jesus condemned the obsession with money as a form of idolatry. He urged his disciples to be detached from the preoccupation of the world with possessions and material security. In its early days the Church took his challenge seriously but this caused problems. In the dramatic story of Ananias and Sapphira, Luke records the tragic end which came to two Christians who sought the reputation of self-denial dishonestly.

2 Duty and need

Throughout Christian history, men acknowledged that giving was a practical expression of commitment. The rich were under pressure to be charitable in their provision for the needy of their own and succeeding generations. Following the pattern of Judaism, tithing was accepted as a practice which provided for the maintenance of the Church's work and its ministry. Emergency situations such as that of a Crusade called forth vast sums of money, usually with the bonus of indulgences in return. There were also times of warm response in support of missionary appeals.

In recent years church people have come to realise that giving has to be more than a sporadic response to emergency appeals, or an occasional contribution when present at an act of worship. They recognise also that giving has to be more continuous than it was in the past, not depending so much on money-raising efforts which drew support from the general public, however helpful this might be. They have come to see that giving has to be planned, prayed-about and covenanted, based not on the need which it is trying to meet, but in the Christian's own inner need to give.

That need has to be aroused by a sense of thanksgiving, for all that we have received from God, from others and not least from our predecessors. Indeed it is not too much to say that if any churches have any measure of financial security today it is largely due to the generosity of past members. Giving should be the natural and spontaneous expression of thanks-giving, and an expression of total commitment. We can remember how Jesus drew attention to this in the Temple. He saw ostentatious donors giving out of the petty cash of their superfluity. He pointed out that the poor widow was making her offering out of 'all the living that she had'. For true giving is always sacrificial.

A story which used to be told at missionary meetings was about a hen and a pig looking at a notice advertising a 'missionary society bacon and egg breakfast'. The hen said: 'Isn't it nice to think that our contributions are supporting such a worthy cause?' The pig replied: 'Yes, but in your case it's a donation. For my family, it means a sacrifice!'

3 *The whole stewardship*

We look at stewardship in terms of money. But it is part of a more comprehensive principle of the stewardship of life as a whole. This is not an academic theory. It is woven into every aspect of living in God's world. It is being recognised as a matter of great importance today. We are concerned over the ecological consequences of man's despoliation of nature. The stewardship of life is involved in the controversies over abortion and euthanasia. It comes into the argument about the gulf between the 'have' and the 'have-not' nations. The progress and unity of a nation depends on the general recognition of the principle that no group and no class has the right to live unto itself. Cain's question: 'Am I my brother's keeper?' is a crucial question of Genesis and is still so for the twentieth century.

Cain is answerable to God. A world that does not believe in God has no sense of accountability to him. This is its lost dimension. If it is obsessed with its own situation, it is not even accountable to posterity. Nevertheless Christianity must witness to its conviction that all nations, classes, races and individuals are accountable to the Father who created and who cares. That witness means that we must know ourselves to be answerable to God ourselves as Christians. That is not a restriction of freedom. It is a liberation. The Prayer Book collect for Peace sums this up superbly when it says of God: 'In whose service is perfect freedom.' This is the way to peace, to find what Paul calls 'The glorious liberty of the children of God'. It is the freedom which God wants his children to enjoy and within it to find happiness in the stewardship of time and talents, of work and relationships—yes, and the stewardship of suffering too.

The status-seekers

There are seven deadly sins. They are Pride, Covetousness, Lust, Envy, Gluttony, Anger and Sloth. According to the Christian ethic the first and most important of these is Pride. But according to the world today it is the most fashionable virtue, at least if one is to judge by the attention given to status. The anxiety about it damages relationships at many levels from the family quarrel to the industrial dispute, where battles over wage-differentials are often at bottom conflicts over status. Its symbols also have great importance attached to them, whether they consist of wall-to-wall carpeting of the executive office or public honours. Pride can have an absurd side to its manifestations, and this was touched on by Jesus when he reacted to what might have been an embarrassing situation.

He had been invited to dine with some Scribes and Pharisees. They had an ulterior motive for inviting him. It happened to be the Sabbath and they watched to see if he would show off his alleged powers by healing a man suffering from the dropsy. Then he would lay himself open to the charge of breaking the law. But he carried the challenge back to them. He reminded them that even on the Sabbath anyone of them would pull his ox or ass out of a ditch in which it had fallen. Surely the healing of a sufferer was a right thing to do, even on the Sabbath? First things first!

Then Jesus proceeded to comment on their own behaviour. He had been amused by their absurd jockeying for positions of honour as they took their places for the meal. He suggested that if invited to a wedding, they would do better to go to the lower seats than to claim the best. How embarrassing it would be to have to give place to someone more important than oneself!

He ended by asserting that God would displace those who exalted themselves and elevate the humble. They might have realised that this was exactly what Jesus was himself doing. For the people to whom he paid particular attention were not the status-figures but the poor, the rejected and the outcast. He dared to say in the Beatitude that the poor would be blessed, for the Kingdom of God would be theirs.

2 Status in the Church

It was no easier for the early Church to take this message to heart than it is for us today. The disciples had to be constantly reminded of the need for humility. On one occasion Jesus set a child among them and told them bluntly that unless they became childlike in simple trust, they had no chance of acceptance by God.

The problem recurred time after time. Serious trouble in Corinth stemmed from the rival claims of parties to superior status. As the charismatic ministries developed, there was conflict between evangelists, healers, people who had the gift of tongues and others. Each group insisted that it was the most essential. Even the Philippians had to be charged to follow the humility of Christ who had 'emptied himself' of his glory and taken the form of a servant. In the Book of Revelation, the Laodiceans were criticised not merely for being lukewarm in devotion but also because of their proud confidence that they lacked nothing in Christianity. But the Epistle of James contains the most caustic criticism of a congregation which offered the seat of honour to the wealthy visitor and told the poor man to sit on the floor—a kind of social discrimination which was all too evident in the nineteenth century and which is not entirely absent in the twentieth!

2 What does status matter?

Status is only of significance if it enables a job to be done more worthily and effectively. Otherwise it becomes ridiculous and even harmful. Christ made this point to the Scribes and Pharisees. It is apparent whenever people claim, or hold on, to positions to which they are not entitled by their own merits. The church officer, the politician, the councillor, or the committee member may demand veneration irrespective of his deserts. He comes to believe in his own importance and indispensability. He may even unconsciously destroy that which he has created by past services. Blessed indeed are those who put the cause higher than themselves—and who know when to resign!

Sometimes we are reluctant to learn what life can teach us about the ephemeral nature of status. Pain and suffering, bereavement and loneliness—these can make painfully clear that all the pomp and circumstance to which we attached so much importance were superficial. We may then realise that our obsession with status has arisen from a deep, though unacknowledged, feeling of insecurity. It is as though a man knows subconsciously that he is acting a part and needs an audience to reassure him. So he may be quick to resent imagined slights and to claim rights to which he is not entitled. What used to be called a 'superiority complex' is really the sign of inferiority and that is a very different thing from humility.

3 *The way of humility*

The difference between the two was clearly recognised by the Apostle Paul. He himself bore insults and humiliation from some of his fellow Christians as well as from Jews and Romans. He has sometimes been criticised for setting out in 2 Corinthians 11.21-28 the catalogue of his sufferings. But this is unfair criticism for the Apostle was simply teaching that suffering and humiliation is of the essence of Christian witness. But, again in writing to Corinth, he claimed a justifiable respect for his Apostleship and his message, for it was not the man but the task, that mattered. And he was absolutely certain that no Church could be truly the Body of Christ unless the relation between all the members was based on humility. There was no room for pride of race, of seniority, of office or of ministry.

The Body of Christ must follow the way of Christ. The Passion narrative describes the last days of Jesus as characterised by a profound yet powerful humility. The two adjectives are not a contradiction. Christ was 'content to be betrayed into the hands of wicked men'. He was passed like a parcel from Pilate to Herod. He was exposed to the derision of the crowd and to manhandling by the troops. Only in response to the direct challenge of the High Priest did he admit to his divine Sonship.

Yet throughout Jesus moved with power and majesty that dominates the scene. He was so utterly unconcerned for himself that he could comfort the women of Jerusalem, the penitent thief and his own mother. He could even pray for the soldiers nailing him to the cross. And one of them could say when all was over, 'Truly this was the Son of God'.

Now, as then, the most profound witness to a world which clutches at power and status to mask its own insecurity, comes from a Christianity which in true humility shows itself 'as having nothing, and yet possessing everything' in Christ.

CHRIST IN ACTION TODAY

Christ the healer

One indication of the character of any nation is its attitude towards the sick. At early stages in man's development sickness was feared as a visitation from evil powers which the patient had offended. For the safety of the tribe, he had to be abandoned or destroyed. Even when any attempt was made to cure him, it would consist largely of the use of magic to control the supernatural forces at work. Gradually a knowledge of herbs and other remedies developed, along with some skills in surgery. But men did not understand the basic causes of disease and epidemics and their relation to diet and sanitation. Disease still bred fear. This prevented men from recognising that however dangerous his condition might be to others, the patient was still of value in his own right.

When Christ began his mission in Galilee, his works of healing drew public attention to him and this might have impeded his real work. On many occasions he tried to keep his healing secret but was frustrated by the crowds bringing their invalid relatives and friends. In his compassion, Jesus healed and went on healing in response to the faith of the invalid or those who brought him. Sometimes, knowing that the sick person needed more than verbal assurance of the cure, Jesus used manual acts. On at least one occasion his treatment was what might nowadays be called psycho-somatic. That was when he diagnosed the physical condition of a sufferer as due to a problem of personality. To the young man stricken with the palsy, he said: 'Your sins are forgiven. Rise and walk.' On another occasion he was challenged to declare whether a man's blindness was due to his own sin or that of his parents. But Jesus would not be led into extraneous issues. He said that the state of the man was above all an opportunity for showing the healing power of God at work.

1 *The command to heal*

The healing of mind and body was a charge which Jesus laid firmly upon his disciples. That was part of the commission entrusted to the seventy when they went out in pairs. It was continued in the early days of the Church with the healing of physical ailments and mental disorders, the latter usually attributed to demon possession. This work of healing was a new and remarkable feature of their religious life. It was quite different from the elaborate sanitary code of the Old Testament. It differed also from the practice of the Gentile world with its mixture of magic and medicine. The Christians saw themselves as instruments of the power of God. Supported by the prayers of the Church, they were concerned to bring the sick person to wholeness of body and mind. For centuries it was the Church which alone exercised any corporate responsibility for the sick. This is reflected in the titles still used of Doctor, originally a doctor of religion, and of Matron who would have been the mother superior of a religious order of which the Sisters were members. The Church continued to fulfil its responsibility for the sick when it went overseas into the mission field. There it pioneered in the research and treatment of tropical diseases, in combating infant mortality and teaching hygiene. But it quickly became evident that medical work could not be isolated from meeting the needs of man in his total environment in terms of education, literacy, housing, welfare and—in recent years—family planning.

2 The way of wholeness

This broad approach shows Christ's concern for the healing of the whole man in his whole society. Jesus could cure the individual sufferer but he also sought to cure the nation of moral and religious sickness. The interdependence of these two aspects of healing has never been more evident than it is today.

Medical science has achieved almost incredible progress in this century. There has been progress also in the acceptance by the State of responsibility for the welfare of every citizen in need of treatment. But every advance seems to be accompanied by new problems such as, for example, those relating to abortion, euthanasia and the prolongation of life. Some of the diseases from which men suffered have almost disappeared. But the complexity of modern life has produced new stress diseases. There is also a heavy toll of casualities through traffic accidents. The general picture almost suggests that civilisation carries within itself a kind of urge towards self-destruction which nullifies its self-development. There is some justification for describing ours as a sick society in desperate need of healing.

3 The way of Christ

It is a mistake to think of Jesus as being concerned only with the healing of the individual to the exclusion of the healing of society. He had a deep compassion for the multitudes 'because they were harassed and helpless, like sheep without a shepherd'. He made no obvious pronouncements about the political or economic situation or about the institution of slavery. But he was acutely aware of the obsession with money which was tantamount to idolatry. He was also critical of the religious establishment which was too introverted to care about the social needs of the people. When he preached about the Kingdom of God he was not presenting a utopian ideal of new forms of government, or of structures of organisation and economics. He was talking about the kind of society in which men valued each other as children of God and put their neighbour's welfare on the same level as their own. It would be free from the insecurity and fear and ruthless competitiveness which are the root causes of social sickness. To make this possible would mean a change of heart rather than a change of politics. This truth he took to the top levels of government and of religion. It is there that the decisions are taken which can help to cause, or to mend, the sick society. His final contribution was to found a Church to be God's instrument of caring and compassion, of challenge and reconciliation.

It was the same message of healing that Jesus brought to the individual whether he was physically or mentally ill, a social misfit or someone who knew that there was something radically wrong with his life. In many cases he asked the person concerned to define and acknowledge what was his particular need, and then to make the response of faith. This was necessary if the cure was to be complete and not merely a temporary alleviation of his condition. In some instances the healed person wanted to dedicate his life immediately to the service of Jesus. Among these is the remarkable man whose story is told in John 9. His gratitude for his sight survived bitter pressurising from the Pharisees.

It has to be recognised that the nature of faith in the situation of sickness is not essentially different from that of faith in normal life. It includes confidence in the skill and ability of those who are ministering to the patient. It requires also the realistic acceptance of the condition which requires treatment. But, as in the rest of one's life, faith means being aware of God's presence and reaching out to him, accepting his will and giving oneself entirely to his love. Then the power of God can get to work on what matters most—the heart and personality of the sufferer. There the real root of the suffering may lie and and its cure may have to begin. There the healing grace of the Father can have the effect of removing the fear and inner conflict which afflict the sufferer in the lonely darkness of the soul.

So we see healing as an essential element in Christ's ministry of wholeness. It was this that he committed to his Church. It was to share and continue his loving and active concern for the body and the mind, as well as the soul, of every man. So its vocation is not fulfilled by worship and evangelism alone. Its witness cannot be limited to standards of personal conduct and judgements on moral issues. Its ministry is redemptive in the fullest sense when it embraces the whole man in his total situation, 'for better, for worse; for richer, for poorer; in sickness and in health; to love and to cherish . . . ' Like a partner in marriage, the Christian is pledged to care for his fellowmen and to convey to them the power of God which makes men whole, and can cure the sickness of their society.

CHRIST IN ACTION TODAY

There is a lad here . . .

If the feeding of the five thousand had been reported in the modern press, we should have had the boy's full name, age, address, school and father's occupation! Instead, he remains one of the many anonymous people of the Gospels who made their individual contribution to Christ's work. It was enough that he was there at a crucial moment. The boy may have been sent out on an errand to buy the loaves and fishes for the family's meal. His curiosity led him to follow the crowd, and to work his way through to the front of it. So he became one of the children of the Bible who played their part in God's purpose.

There were many of these. One was Samuel, entrusted by his devout mother Hannah to be brought up at the great sanctuary of Shiloh. Despite the weakness and corruption of the priesthood there, Samuel grew up unharmed and learned to be obedient to the call of God. When the time was ripe, Samuel was to unite the nation and lay the foundation of the monarchy. He was eventually to anoint David whose boyhood experience had given him the courage to stand up to every enemy, and the faith which was to sustain him when he became king.

And of course Christianity is permanently indebted to Luke for his glimpse of the boyhood of Jesus. In the Temple he showed his desire to know the truth about religion and his awareness of his special relationship with God.

1 *The school of youth*

The study of biography has made us realise how the events of youth affect achievement in adult life. One thinks of David Livingstone working in a cotton mill, seizing every moment to educate himself and laying the foundation for the whole-hearted commitment which took him to Africa. Florence Nightingale may have seemed a conventional young daughter of a wealthy family, charitably visiting the homes of the poor in sickness. But that was the beginning of her profound concern for people in trouble which was eventually to lead her to reform the whole medical service of the Army. Albert Schweitzer followed the same pattern. A brilliant young musician reaching high honours in one profession, he went on to do the same in the realm of theology. Then he trained as a doctor to fulfil his true vocation in Africa. By what he did, and even more by what he was, Schweitzer's example stamped itself upon the world's attention.

There have been many other examples of youthful dedication to a cause by people, outside Christendom, who have achieved world-wide reputations. In 1848 at the age of thirty, Karl Marx published the Communist Manifesto and laid the foundations of an ideology which today controls the lives of one-third of the world's population. Forty years later there arrived at London University a twenty-one year old Indian student who was interested in getting to the root of ethical and religious beliefs. As Mahatma Gandhi, he became the most influential figure India has produced for centuries.

It is impossible to identify any significant factors common to all such people. But what is evident is at quite an early age they became aware of some dominant concern to which they gave themselves with a developing single-mindedness. There is no 'average age' at which this happens but we must recognise that it can do so earlier than might be expected.

Some years ago at a church conference, there were four missionaries on the platform. They were an archbishop, a priest, a doctor and an agriculturalist. They were asked when they had first become aware, however indistinctly, of a call to serve overseas. Each gave the same answer—thirteen years of age. The idea of their giving service overseas might have come from their home, church or school—although two of the speakers acknowledged that theirs had not been a Christian home. There may have been some other influence at work. Possibly, like Samuel, there had been a moving of the Spirit preparing them for future ministry.

2 *The crucible of the family*

That the child of today is the adult of tomorrow, is an obvious platitude. It states a truth which is dangerous to ignore. We are concerned about the quality of life to be enjoyed in the future by our children. We want to do something constructive about it in terms of planning, economics, scientific development and security. We have to be equally concerned about the kind of people who will inhabit tomorrow's world—that is about our children themselves. We have to ask ourselves what we are doing to prepare them for it, and where we begin.

It is undeniable that the most significant preparation is still that which takes place in the family, even though today it may be in a state of confusion. This is implied even in the criticisms heaped upon it. The failures of children are attributed to parental indifference, repression, indulgence, materialism, irresponsibility, infidelity . . . and so on. The family is always blamed.

Yet when a family breaks down this often happens because it has succumbed to the pressures put upon it by society itself. Society condemns the parent who tries to teach his children the meaning of discipline and of self-discipline. It houses its families in situations where community life is impossible. It steadily whittles away parental choice and responsibility in education. It discourages religious teaching in schools while pretending to protect it. It laments the increase of promiscuity and violence among the young while tolerating displays of pornography in newspaper shops and displays of violence on the mass media. These harmful influences upon the family undo the good which the state tries to offer through the social services. It is content to spend millions more on remedial treatment than on preventive measures.

3 What of the church?

It is not enough to blame society for what is happening to the family. Churches and Christians are part of that society. They have to look at their own family life and its possible contribution to the solution of the contemporary problem. In an equally difficult situation, Paul valued the Christian household as a bulwark of the Church and at the same time as the base of its outreach to the world. He saw its unity as dependent on its being 'one in Christ' and so giving a new meaning to marriage and parenthood. In this context questions of status, authority and dependence became of secondary importance. What mattered far more was a partnership in love, with each other and with Christ.

This is still the vocation of the Christian family. When it is fulfilled, then the children have a chance of realising their own vocation in the widest sense. They come to see what it means to be a husband, wife, father, mother, or citizen or even a responsible member of the human family. They learn something about the relative worth of money and possessions. They learn too the value of themselves and other people with whom they are in any kind of relationship. And one hopes that they grow to understand the meaning of integrity and of truth by which to measure the ideas pressed upon them by the world.

Of course the home is not the child's only experience. He will move on from it to be influenced by the outlook and code of other young people, of his school or his place of work or study. There may well be conflict between the ideas and values which he has learned in his home and those which he acquires outside it. They may indeed have the greater influence upon him. But the contribution which his family has made to his development is not likely to be wholly displaced if it helped him to become a real person and to find meaning for his life.

And this is true of what he has learned about God in his home. There is no obvious cause-and-effect principle about this. There are many young people brought up in Christian homes—in the best sense of the word and not a merely puritanical interpretation—who reject the religion of their youth. In the same way, there are many young people brought up in godless families who find their way to Christ despite positive opposition from their relatives. Jesus himself warned that his teaching would bring not peace but a sword, and significantly he forecast that this would cut into family life first.

The Christian family has to accept the joys as well as the trials of being 'in Christ', the happiness of giving as well as that of receiving, the burden of failure and the glory of achievement. Its reward is the unity which Christ gives by drawing each member to himself. Its witness is not one of static piety or cosy four-walled togetherness—but of growth in love and service as it grows in grace.

CHRIST IN ACTION TODAY

The voice of the people

Never has public opinion received so much attention as it does today. Millions are spent on giving it information by advertising paid for by governments, political parties and commercial firms. Public relations have become almost an industry in itself. One of the functions of education is said to be that of producing an educated public opinion.

Its analysis has also become something of an industry. New commercial products are launched after considerable market research. Politicians and newspapers engage in expensive opinion polls. Although the consequent forecasts frequently turn out to be mistaken, this is usually blamed not on the methods employed but on the unpredictability of human nature. The public also tends to be blamed when complaints are made about the preponderance of violence, sensationalism or sex in the mass media. For the usual defence is that this is only 'giving the public what it wants'.

Mass communication along these lines has become part of the life of society, rapid and extensive in its impact however ephemeral in its results. Yet centuries ago when these methods were not available, public opinion seems to have become well informed and active, even if slower in its operation. The international reputation of a saint, the spread of orthodox or heretical religious opinion, the kind of enthusiasm which initiated the Crusades, the growth of the Reformation, the rise of socialism, the extension of communism—these are but a few examples of movements in public opinion which changed the lives of millions, although they began on a small scale.

1 Christ and the public

The importance of public opinion runs as a thread through the Gospels. At one stage, the multitude wanted to make Jesus king. Later, those who welcomed him with Hosannas may well have been in the crowd that cried 'Crucify!' But Jesus would never have praised or condemned either demand. He fully realised what lay behind them. He knew how the multitude could be manipulated by the unscrupulous.

One of the most interesting examples of Christ's approach to this problem is that of his comment on John the Baptist as recorded in Luke 7 and Matthew 11. The Forerunner was in prison. He was perturbed by the reports which he had heard about Jesus' mission. It must have seemed to him to lack the decisiveness of the One who was to denounce evil and bring judgement on sinners. There was a wistfulness in the question:

'Are you he that should come or are we to go on expecting someone else?' Jesus sent the messengers back to report not only on his miracles but, even more important, that 'the poor have the Gospel preached to them'. This was in the true prophetic tradition.

2 *You can't win!*

Then Jesus turned to the crowd. He asked them how had they expected the Forerunner to behave—like a reed shaken by the wind or like a palace courtier?

With masterly irony Jesus commented that there was no pleasing that generation. They were like children playing weddings and funerals, expecting others to dance to their changing tune. They had dismissed John as a madman because of his ascetic way of life. They complained that Jesus appeared to indulge himself with the good things of life and consorted with sinners. They were as inconsistent as they were irrational. They rejected both the Baptist and Christ because they did not conform to the popular image of a prophet and a messiah. Only those who were children of God had the sense to look beyond the man to his message and true character.

3 *Weddings and funerals*

This was true not only of the reaction of the outside world to the agents of God. It could happen within the Church. Paul had to fight many a battle to make his converts understand the significance and authority of his own apostleship. This is not unknown in the Church today, in respect of what a congregation expects of the ordained ministry. Despite the growth of understanding of the responsibilities of the laity, it is still dangerously easy to expect the clergy and ministers to be the 'the Church', particularly when action and witness are expected. But they are sometimes cautioned against embarrassing the Church: 'He must not preach politics', as if politics were not part of God's world. He must not be 'too spiritual', or 'too worldly', 'unsociable', 'too interested in outsiders' and so on. Paul could say that he had to become 'all things to all men so that I might by all means save some'. But he did that not so as to please everybody, nor did it obscure his first responsibility to be a man of God.

In fact, one has to ask if a congregation gives the same priority as did Paul to the minister's being a man of God. Their opinion on this matter indicates what is their concept of the nature of the Church itself. It shows what they think of vocation, not least of their own vocation as Christians. One of the signs of progress in Christendom has been the growing concern to discover what it means to be the whole people of God. As 1 Peter 2.9, shows clearly, the priesthood of all believers is not a question of the legal status of the laity, but the basis of the missionary obligation of the whole Church.

4 Communicating the truth

Jesus had to accept the risk of being misunderstood and rejected. He warned his disciples that they would have to do the same, in their proclamation of the Gospel. This has been true of Christianity throughout history and never more so than today. At times it means having to challenge and expose wrong ideas, however powerfully supported by vested interests and passively received by the public.

The nursery tale of the Emperor's new clothes is a parable about this situation. The king was fooled by unscrupulous charlatans, into wearing invisible clothes. His sycophantic courtiers did not dare to contradict him. The delusion was shattered by the voice of a child, who laughed at the king because he was naked.

The delusions and myths of man need at times to be frankly ridiculed. They have to be challenged by those who refuse to accept face values and ask awkward questions about ends and means. As Shakespeare wrote:

'O! while you live, tell the truth, and shame the devil!'

But who is to question public opinion and those who would manipulate it? To answer that, we might first ask who informs public opinion. Politicians, educationalists, journalists, broadcasters, writers, leaders of industrial and other organisations . . .

the list seems endless and yet all together the informers probably constitute less than one in a thousand of the total population. There is therefore a comparatively small number of
people who, for good or ill, influence the ideas, the values and
the decisions of their fellow men.

That gives some ground for hope. It also asks the Christian
what part he or she plays at any level in communicating the
truth to those with whom he is in direct personal contact.
That must begin in the primary area of communication which
so far we have not mentioned. This is the home. This is the
place where attitudes and values and relationships are formed
which will have an important influence on the child as he
grows into adult life. It should also be a kind of laboratory
where all the influences bearing upon him in the world outside
can be looked at and tested. For it is in the family that we have
to learn the difference between right and wrong, and to learn
to think for ourselves objectively and responsibly.

This is the kind of growth towards spiritual and moral and
intellectual maturity which Paul put before his converts. He
saw it as essential to their life in the Church. But it was equally
essential as part of the service which the Church could give to
the world.

CHRIST IN ACTION TODAY

Apologies not accepted

Anyone who has ever been a member of a committee knows
how a long list of apologies for absence can get a meeting off
to a dispiriting start. Some may be unavoidable. Another may
indicate that its sender cannot be bothered to attend and gives
an excuse, rather than a genuine reason, for absence. The
obligations of membership may receive a low priority in his
scale of values and he feels no personal commitment. That

may be why in the north of England sending an apology of this kind is bluntly described as 'giving back word'.

1 *Invitation to a banquet*

This subject of commitment occurs in the New Testament on a number of occasions. In Luke 14, Jesus told the story of a banquet to which the guests had accepted invitations. At the last moment they 'gave back word'. On the surface, their excuses seemed adequate. Two pleaded business and one, matrimony. None of the three attached any importance to the wishes or convenience of his host. None felt that he was committed in any way, or that his new obligations could be fulfilled later.

The host was well aware of the flimsiness of the excuses. In the ordinary way, he would have felt hurt and that would be the end of the matter. Convention would expect him to have the 'good manners' to ignore the bad manners of his guests. But Christ was using this parable at a deeper level than that of ordinary social intercourse. He was employing the theme of the banquet which was familiar as a description of the Messianic joys which God had prepared for Israel. This he applied to a parable of judgement. The Jews had rejected the invitation to the Kingdom proclaimed by Christ. So God would welcome in their place the social misfits and outcasts, and even the Gentiles. The Chosen People had rejected God's summons and chosen other priorities, refusing to honour their covenant.

There were others who would reject God's offer. Jesus knew that his hearers would do so, and even some of his closest followers. He warned that those who had put their hands to the plough and regretted their commitment would not be worthy of the Kingdom. John's Gospel records a critical occasion when Jesus spoke of himself as the living bread and the flesh which his followers must eat. The very idea was anathema to Jews and many of those who had believed in him fell away. As the months went by there must have been others who did the same, particularly as he appeared to come increasingly into conflict with the Jewish authorities. At the end, the over-confident Peter denied him. Judas betrayed him. The rest foresook him before he came to the Cross. When it came to Easter, he had to rebuild his Church out of a body of men who had first to be forgiven for their failure to keep faith with him.

3 Keep faith

Spiritual commitment, however, is more than giving one's word and keeping it. It means giving one's life a new dimension based upon entrusting oneself entirely to the will of God. In the remarkable eleventh chapter of the Epistle to the Hebrews, the unknown writer ranges back through the Old Testament. He quotes many examples of people who demonstrated the faith which is 'the assurance of things hoped for, the conviction of things not seen'. They are 'the cloud of witnesses' surrounding modern Christians.

The Old Testament has many instances of apparently deliberate contrast between men of faith and obedience and contemporaries who lacked these qualities. These parallels of religious strength and weakness include such pairs as Abraham and Lot, Samuel and Saul, Elijah and Ahab, Isaiah and Ahaz, Jeremiah and Zedekiah. In each case, the first named is not necessarily sinless but is sound in his relationship with God. He is what the Old Testament calls *tamim*—this is, perfect in the wholeness of his commitment. The others are irresolute in faith and weak in obedience. And their weakness leads them to sin. This is one of the facts of life. For disaster and suffering are caused more often by weakness than by strength. This is one of the themes exemplified in Shakespeare's *Hamlet*.

Jesus put it another way when, before performing a miracle, he would sometimes ask the question: 'Do you believe that I can do this?' The positive answer was more than an expression of hope. It meant a leap of faith across pragmatism, across material 'proof' that such a thing was impossible It was the same for the disciples. They may have been sustained in the early part of their discipleship by the hope that the Kingdom was to be achieved quickly and painlessly. All the signs pointed this way when Christ's mission was meeting with so remarkable and successful a response throughout Galilee. They found it hard to accept the possibility that the Kingdom would come only after the rejection, suffering and death of their Master. This was the banquet to which they were being called, not one of immediate glory. Their commitment was to a purpose and vocation whose consequences could not be foreseen. The depth of their faith and the quality of their love would determine how they eventually fulfilled it.

3 No conditions

The willingness to make a commitment without conditions implies that the person who is asking for it inspires confidence and a sense of security. This is not easy to achieve today when people tend to have little confidence in their fellow men and even less in ideals. As one dramatist wrote recently: 'There are no good causes left.' This does not mean that people are not willing to give themselves wholly to some cause with which they can fully identify themselves. A very demanding commitment is characteristic of some of the sects on the extreme fringe of Christianity. It has also been prominent in the spread of Communism. This suggests that there is in human nature a willingness to respect commitment and to give it when the demands are far-reaching. These demands may be irrational, inhumane and ruthless. But they give meaning and purpose to the lives of those who accept them. The tragedy is that sooner or later their very failure to have any real respect for human nature can cause disillusionment and the last state is worse than the first.

Yet Christianity has to recognise this receptiveness in man's nature and make use of it for the right reasons, as Christ himself did. It is an area which tends to be neglected. The Church has become self-conscious about itself, aware as it is of its past mistakes and present weaknesses. But that does not mean that it has any right to be self-conscious about its Gospel, or about its own commitment to recruit men for the Kingdom of God. Whether it likes this or not, the Church has to evangelise, so presenting Christ as to win the response of faith. It may be content to do otherwise, to concentrate on its internal life and its external social or political activism. If so, it is relapsing into the heresy about which Paul warned the Galatians, and Luther challenged the Church in his day, that is the heresy of preaching a Gospel of works and not of faith.

To be entitled to preach commitment, a Church and a Christian must live by it. So as Christians we must examine the degree of our own commitment to the Church in two respects. One is of course the faith and obedience we give to our vocation as clergy and laity. Worship, prayer, sacraments, the scriptures, sharing in work and fellowship and financial support—all these are aspects of membership in which our commitment ought to be responsible and dependable. And it ought to be both joyous and growing throughout our lives. For the keynote of one's religious life, if it is really one of commitment to Christ, should be one of growth, not of static limitation.

But commitment does not stop there. It spreads into our own homes and affects the nature of our marriage and parenthood, our relations with our neighbours, the exercise of our citizenship and our involvement in the world. Paul dared to tell the Corinthians this: 'We are ambassadors for Christ, God making his appeal through us.' But perhaps most of us would find it easier to think of ourselves as God's uncommercial travellers!

CHRIST IN ACTION TODAY

Show me a penny

Modern translations of the Bible sometimes give a new edge to a familiar quotation. The Authorised Version of Matthew 6.21 has: 'For where your treasure is, there will your heart be also.' In the New English Bible this is: 'For where your wealth is, there will your heart be also.' The latter reminds us sharply

that Jesus had quite a lot to say about money and its significance for religious life.

The best known instance is the occasion when his opponents tried to trap Jesus with a question about money. They asked if Jews ought to pay taxes to Caesar. They thought they had him cornered. If he said yes, then he would offend the Jews, who bitterly resented having to pay taxes to the foreign oppressor. If he said no, he would be immediately in serious trouble with the Roman authorities.

Jesus asked to be shown a denarius. This silver coin represented the day's wage of a labourer. It was the most used coin in Roman currency, in value one-twenty-fifth of the aereus or golden 'sovereign'. It was issued by the Emperor, not by the Senate. No orthodox Jew would carry it for it bore the head of Caesar with the Latin inscription 'Tiberius Caesar, son of the deified Augustus'.

Our Lord asked whose image and superscription the coin bore. They replied: 'Caesar's'. He said something which probed far deeper than any question of paying taxes: 'Render to Caesar the things that are Caesar's, and to God the things that are God's.' And they were silent, perhaps realising that he had challenged them with a far-reaching principle, drawn from the common coin whose name the A.V. translates as a 'penny'.

1 *Image and superscription*

The modern penny is worth far less than was the denarius of our Lord's time. But it has a curiously theological inscription. It bears the face and name of the reigning sovereign. Around the rim are the letters D.G. REG. F.D. The first five letters mean that by the grace of God the monarch reigns. The F.D. describes the sovereign as Defender of the Faith. That takes us back to the time of Henry VIII. The title was conferred upon him for his defence of the seven sacraments against the teaching of Martin Luther. The title has been carried by British monarchs since 1544.

So this inscription says that the sovereign is so by the grace of God and is responsible for the defence of the faith.

2 Vocation and grace

The link between vocation and grace is not an academic theological point. It has a direct bearing upon our manner of life. When we say that by the grace of God we are what we are, we might take this to mean that we are not really responsible for our situation. This takes us back to the days when men viewed life as predestined in every detail. The fortunate could thank God that all was well with them, and expect others to accept unquestioningly any misfortunes which came their way. This is illustrated in Mrs Alexander's famous lines:

'The rich man in his castle
  The poor man at his gate
God made them, high or lowly,
  And order'd their estate.'

We no longer assume that our work, for example, can always be regarded as a vocation. There are many forms of modern employment that are meaningless, frustrating and dehumanising. One can hardly regard such jobs as being God's will for the person who has to perform them, however much he may count on the grace of God to help him.

But we have swung to the opposite extreme of thinking that we live in a kind psychological determinism which excludes both grace and responsibility. A student took home a poor report and asked his parent: 'Father, what's wrong with me; is it my heredity or my environment?' He was only using an argument common nowadays. It is not unlike transferring the responsibility of one's life to astrology. For here again men come to think that ultimately their lives are determined by forces beyond their control. So they are not to blame.

Of course Christian common sense helps us to realise that our decisions are influenced by factors both within and outside ourselves. We can only marvel at the shallow optimism of W. E. Henley's words:

'I am the master of my fate
I am the captain of my soul.'

We believe that it is we ourselves who have to accept responsibility for dealing with these factors. And the grace of God is there to help us not only to be what we are—but to become what we can become. In the words of the television programme: 'This is *your* life'.

3 *Grace and faith*

Living by grace is inextricably bound up with living by faith. Every man lives by some kind of belief whether it is about himself, about other people or about God, however positive or vague it may be. This is especially evident when he enters into a close relationship with someone in marriage. Its success or failure may depend on his beliefs about love, sex, faithfulness or partnership and about the respective roles of husband and wife. His ideas may be difficult to put into words. But taken together they make up a kind of faith which embodies itself in his behaviour and development.

Now that is true of the kind of faith we are discussing. It is more than a set of ideas, however religious. It is the movement of the whole personality acting out those ideas, growing by experience, reinforced by the experience of others, reaching towards God. For God reveals the truth on which faith is based and gives us the grace to understand it and grow in it.

It is this living faith, both personal and corporate, which the Church and the Christian is called upon to defend. It is more than a set of ideas. It is the experience of God as we have known it through the Bible, through twenty centuries of Christianity and through using God-given reason. It is founded not only on God's revelation of himself within the Church in the widest sense. It looks to the world outside and sees God at work there too.

This is the glorious dynamic faith described in Ephesians 3.17-19 as the 'breadth and length and height and depth' of Christ dwelling in the heart. This is what we have to defend—not an ideology, not a social doctrine, not even 'civilisation' as such. It is a conviction about the reality of God and about man's nature, needs and potential under God.

This was the faith of Christ. But he did not defend it, if by that one means that he was on the defensive about it. He proclaimed it and he lived by it. And that is what the defence of the faith means today. Too often Christians are self-conscious and tongue-tied when Christianity is under attack or even the subject of open-minded inquiry by the world. The television programme, the conversation in the canteen, the committee meeting, the political assembly, the encounter with the door-step salesman of some strange cult, the questioning from the child in the home, the youngsters arguing in the youth club, the hospital patient who asks 'Why me?' ... there are many situations of which Paul would have said 'be instant in season and out of season ... unfailing in patience and teaching'. For our concern is to 'render unto God the things that are God's'. That is above all humanity itself, sinful but saveable, the crown of creation and its greatest problem, but nevertheless the object of the love of God.

Dei Gratia ... *Fidei Defensor* ... grace and faith in action together.

CHRIST IN ACTION TODAY

Thank God for me!

'Now children, let us thank God that we are not like that nasty Pharisee,' the Sunday School teacher concluded after telling her class the story of the Pharisee and the Publican in Luke 18. Her unconscious self-righteousness was Pharisaic in itself! But we too miss the point of our Lord's parable if we lightly condemn the Pharisee as a hypocrite. He belonged to a class which had much to commend it.

The name of the Pharisees meant 'the separated ones'. They sincerely believed that their separation was God's will for them. They came from all classes and were mainly laymen. Their influence spread from the synagogues which they developed as centres of study and charitable works as well as of worship. The ordinary folk greatly respected them for the austerity of their lives and their resistance to pagan influences.

Pharisees based their religious beliefs and practices upon the Law of Moses. But they gave almost equal prominence to the oral tradition of precepts and regulations which they had built up around it. Unlike the Sadducees, they believed in a resurrection and judgement after death. It has also to be remembered that according to Acts 5, it was a Pharisee, Gamaliel, who spoke up for the apostles before the Sanhedrin.

There was much to admire about their beliefs and their way of life. What Christ criticised, as in Matthew 23.23 was the externalism and formalism in their keeping of the Law. He was also opposed to their burdening the common people with many additional restrictions. He pointed out that they were liable to be self-righteous and to neglect the justice and mercy which lay at the heart of the Law as God intended it.

1 *Two men at prayer*

In this parable Jesus was talking about the right attitude to God in prayer. He depicted the Pharisee as the 'self-made man'. He congratulated himself that he was not like other men— particularly the Publican behind him. He reminded God that he fulfilled his religious obligations fully and punctiliously. But he had no sense of need for he had no sense of sin.

The other man was a Publican. In the eyes of the Jewish world he was a traitor to his country. For the sake of profit he had allowed himself to be· the instrument of extortion and oppression. The parable says nothing about this. It concentrates upon his attitude to God and to himself. The Publican in humility did not even raise his eyes. In penitence he beat his breast and asked God for the forgiveness which he had no hope of receiving from men. He knew that in their eyes he was a sinner—just as the Pharisee knew himself to be regarded as a saint. Because he acknowledged his desperate need for forgiveness, the Publican went home 'justified', in the right relationship with God.

2 A Publican's prayer

It has been suggested that the Publican's prayer is dangerously simple. It is all too easy to acknowledge that one is a sinner when one is in a passing mood of regret. True penitence needs to make the effort to be specific about the ways in which one sins against God or against one's neighbour. It is like the difference between 'not feeling too well' and accepting the possibility that there is something radically amiss with our health. The wrong kind of penitence can be as superficial as the satisfaction of the Pharisee, who could avoid searching self-examination by assuring himself that he was better than other men.

Nevertheless, the Publican's prayer is based on the right attitude of the soul. This accepts the fact of sin in one's own life. It does not excuse it or try to explain it away as mere weakness of no great importance. And along with that goes the recognition that the only possible remedy lies in the forgiveness of God which can liberate us from ourselves and enable us to make a clean start. The psalmist wrote:

'Create in me a clean heart, O God, and put a new and steadfast spirit within me.'

Such a prayer, however, would seem to be out of date today. For the sense of sin receives little prominence in contemporary Christian thought. This may be because we have too readily assumed that psychology has exposed—or exploded—the myth of sin. It is true that much that was formerly categorised as sinful has been shown to originate from instincts that are in themselves neutral. We understand that feelings of guilt may be traced back to the tensions of childhood. We recognise that the sense of sin may be engendered by the conflict of loyalties and responsibilities. But all these helps to the understanding of the working of the mind do not eliminate the responsibility of the personality for its own character and decisions. And in this, sin is a reality, for it has been described as 'The purposeful disobedience of the creature to the known will of God'. That is why the greatest sin, according to the Bible, is the deliberate choice of evil rather than good, of darkness rather than light. This is the 'sin against the Holy Ghost'. It is when we acknowledge this, that we begin to move towards the healing and integration which only God's forgiveness can provide.

3   The end-product

It was the man with the sense of sin who went out in a right relationship with God. This is equally true of the Church. Sometimes the modern Church gives the impression of coming to God with a measure of self-righteousness, as if it were saying: 'God, look at all our excellent works, our active fellowship, our new structures of organisation, our social outreach, our new ways of worship, our ecumenical developments, our new image . . . ' All these are good, as were the obligations which the Pharisee could claim to have fulfilled. And yet there may be something missing, of which a sense of sin is but a part.

Perhaps this is the sense of God. One wonders whether even in the Temple the Pharisee had any real awareness of God other than as a projection of himself. In terms of the definition of sin we have already given, the 'known will of God' was unknown to him. That was where the trouble began.

So it is with the Church. Its first task is to wait upon God and patiently to seek his will. That may mean looking at our ideas and plans from an entirely different angle. We must ask about each of them if this is really what God is wanting us to do. All too often one feels that the Holy Spirit can only get into the business of church meetings under the last item of Any Other Business on the agenda. Likewise when we look back on the past, we might do so recognising where and why we have made mistakes, and where our work has born fruit by the grace of God. What we are looking for is evidence of 'justification'—not in the sense of justifying our policies but, as in terms of this parable, of our having a right relationship with God. For this is the purpose of the Church itself as it is of the life of the Christian, that we should be what he would have us be, live as he would have us live and love as he would have us love.

CHRIST IN ACTION TODAY

No vote of thanks

It was the annual meeting of the charitable society. There was an excellent report of the work done during the past year by the staff and a few voluntary workers. Some of the beneficiaries also were present, to show their gratitude in person. The statement of income and expenditure was reassuring. All was going well. Then one of those awkward individuals who seem to enjoy throwing a spanner into the works, made a revolutionary proposal. He suggested that the society should give up publishing a list of subscribers, or omit any indication of the amounts they had contributed. He felt sure that if they had the cause really at heart, they would not mind this omission. In any case, he said, the present practice was unrealistic. The small contributions from some people might well represent a greater proportion of their income than was the case with some of the wealthier subscribers. For a moment there was silence and it was as though the angels hovered hopefully. Then the suggestion was brushed aside with all the arguments one might expect. They were summed up by the chairman's final words: 'After all, people are only human.'

1 No bonus for piety

'People are only human'—but sometimes Jesus appeared to expect his followers to be more than human, particularly about religious obligations. In the Sermon on the Mount he gave this warning: 'Beware of practising your piety before men in order to be seen by them; for then you will have no reward from your Father which is in heaven.' He applied this to almsgiving and prayer, two of the most important religious duties among the Jews. He said that his hearers must not draw attention to themselves when giving alms. They were not to offer prayers in public so as to make an impression on passers-by. When people did this, 'They have their reward' already and must not expect the additional reward of the favour of God as a bonus. He went even further, telling his disciples that when giving alms they should be so utterly lacking in self-interest that it was as though their left hand did not know what their right hand was doing. It was sufficient that God should know what they were doing.

He demanded an equal disinterestedness about love: 'If you love only those who love you, what reward have you? Do not even the tax gatherers do the same? You must therefore be perfect, as your heavenly Father is perfect.'

This sounds like a superhuman standard of perfection and another example of the unrealistic idealism of which Christ is sometimes accused. Yet it was consistent with the rest of his teaching about conduct with its emphasis on motivation. He had taught that what mattered more than the outward act of murder and adultery was the inward disposition of hate or lust. He was now applying this theme to the positive aspects of outwardly virtuous conduct. Its test lay in the inner motive which must be the unqualified love of God and man with no thought of self-interest.

2 Grace is free

Jesus was talking to an audience composed of people for whom rules of conduct, with associated rewards or punishments, were an accepted element in their tradition and way of life. It was clear and definite and understandable. It gave a code of behaviour which unified them. Jewish Christians had been brought up to believe that this was the will of God and that obedience to this code gave them, as it were, something of a claim upon the favour of God as a fair reward for good works. They sincerely believed that newly converted Gentiles should conform to the same Law to be saved. To argue otherwise was to encourage religious anarchy and to deny the whole purpose of God through the ages.

The man who did most to overcome the barrier of this tradition to the Christian mission to the world, was himself a Jew, Paul. He started from his own experience. He acknowledged that he had been completely undeserving of the revelation of Christ on the Damascus road. He had been saved by the free grace of God on which he had absolutely no claim. That was the ground of his apostleship and that same grace was available to all who made the response of faith.

3 *What do we deserve?*

This Jewish-Christian controversy which colours much of the New Testament may seem remote from our contemporary concerns. But the problem of virtue and reward exists in every age. The triumph of evil worried the Psalmist as it did the disciples and the writer of Revelation. It was tempting to question the providence of God when goodness appeared to be rewarded only by failure or persecution, while wickedness prospered. One way out of the difficulty was along the familiar 'pie in the sky' line which counselled patient endurance of suffering here on the promise of glory hereafter. But this has never been wholly convincing, particularly to those who believed that if God was to be consistent, then his justice must be apparent in this present life. A broader viewpoint looked critically at the apparent success of the ungodly and saw that it was often temporary and ephemeral. It also looked at the life of goodness and found that while it did not seem to be rewarded with prosperity in material terms, it could bring its own rewards in terms of peace of mind, integrity and purpose. In that sense, virtue was its own reward with the additional factor, in the religious context, of the knowledge that it was fulfilling the will of God. The Church could come to see that by following this way, it was identifying itself with its Master and must accept the reward of the Cross. So doing, Christianity eventually won respect from a world which came to recognise the shallowness of its own rewards of power and status and pleasure. It warmed to the kind of witness which has been so cogently described in the prayer of St Ignatius Loyola:

'Teach us, good Lord, to serve thee as thou deservest; to give and not to count the cost; to fight and not to heed the wounds; to toil and not to seek for rest; to labour and not to ask for any reward save that of knowing that we do thy will.'

4 *What's in it for me?*

This might be thought of as asking too much of human nature, even of the ordinary Christian. It is understandable that when we are asked to commit ourselves to some task, we should put the question: 'What's in it for me?' Ordinarily the emphasis lies on the first word—'What'—in relation to material benefits or other advantages. But when the question is put in a Christian context, the stress is on the last word: 'Me'. Then I have to ask myself what kind of a person I am, in my heart, in my relationships, in my needs and perhaps in my abilities. So the question turns itself upside-down and becomes one of my giving rather than of my receiving.

When Jesus called his disciples he made no promises. As they shared his life, they accepted a way of insecurity and uncertainty. Once or twice they asked him about their future, as in Mark 10.28's record of an implied query from Peter. They had left everything and they would receive, he promised, a host of new relationships but also persecutions—and eternal life. He made the same offer to the rich young man. So it would seem that this is the real reward of the Christian life, this eternal life, a quality of being, a fundamental purpose, a deep relationship with God. This is what Paul described as 'the peace of God which passes all understanding will keep your hearts and your minds in Christ Jesus'. This peace was the living experience of the early Church and it is spoken of in every single epistle in the New Testament. As early as the beginning of the second century there is evidence that in the eucharistic liturgy Christians always greeted each other with the Pax and the words: 'The peace of the Lord be always with you.'

For Christ's peace is the bond of unity, the power of wholeness and the reward of faith. It is the experience of the life eternal here and now.

Who isn't my neighbour?

One of the world's best known stories was told to a man who had the wrong idea of the man next door. It happened because a lawyer thought that one had the right to eternal life if one discharged due obligations to God and to one's neighbour. The first was clear to him. On the second he challenged Jesus to define the term 'neighbour'.

But Jesus had what must have seemed to some people an exasperating habit. Instead of answering a question directly, he would counter with another question or some illustration which put the whole issue in an entirely different context. In this case, he told the story of the Good Samaritan (Luke 10. 30-37). The parable had a double-edged challenge to the lawyer. Its hero was a Samaritan. The lawyer could not even bring himself to use the hated name when admitting this fact. Secondly, he had asked the question as to the identity of his neighbour, as if the neighbour were bound to be the object of his own charity. But in the parable the passive recipient became the active giver and vice versa. The lawyer had to identify himself with the victim of the robbers. He was the one who needed the neighbour.

Once more, Jesus was taking a conventional idea to which men paid lip-service and turning it inside out. The result was a new revelation about human relations. Neighbourliness became a mutual involvement between people who have to give and to receive from each other. Their contact might be casual. They might share no ties of blood, class, common interest or even relgion. For the word neighbour literally means 'the nearest one'—not 'the dearest one'. And this is exactly the problem of neighbourliness in the modern world.

1 *Counsel of perfection?*

Even within Christendom there has been a continuing tension between the broad and the narrow definitions of neighbourliness. The latter has predominated when men have concentrated upon the 'otherness' of their fellow men, as heretics, enemies, political opponents or the like. From time to time efforts have been made to restore the balance. One of these is in the now-neglected passage in the Catechism of the Book of Common Prayer. The answer to the question 'What is thy duty towards thy neighbour?' is this:

'My duty towards my neighbour, is to love him as myself, and to do to all men, as I would they should do unto me: To love, honour and succour my father and mother: To honour and obey the King, and all that are put in authority under him: To submit myself to all my governors, teachers, spiritual pastors and masters: To order myself lowly and reverently to all my betters: To hurt no body by word nor deed: To be true and just in all my dealings: To bear no malice nor hatred in my heart: To keep my hands from picking and stealing, and my tongue from evil-speaking; To keep my body in temperance, soberness, and chastity: Not to covet nor desire other men's goods: but to learn and labour truly to get mine own living, and to do my duty in that state if life, unto which it shall please God to call me.'

2 Love and duty

At first glance, this sixteenth century definition seems hopelessly out of date, with its overtones of meek submissiveness to a host of 'superiors'. Yet when we examine its clauses in the context of our contemporary problems of personality and relationships, they say something challenging to our complacent superiority.

To love my neighbour as myself means giving him the same benefit of the doubt, the same tolerance, the same forgiveness that I would claim for myself. To do to all men as I would they should do to me, is quite different from the negative principle which says that I should not do to others what I would not wish them to do to me. It calls for positive kindness, in place of vaguely benevolent indifference.

'To love, honour and succour my father and mother'—set

that in the context of the neglect of old people by their relatives, and we touch on a considerable social problem.

'To be true and just in all my dealings' ranges from the quality of workmanship to income tax returns, in its wide applications. It would strengthen in commerce and industry the old principle that 'my word is my bond'—and make a fair amount of the work of the law courts superfluous. Honesty in word and deed, chastity and self-control, refusal to covet the possessions or status of others—is it only wishful thinking to suggest that returning to these principles of personal conduct might do much to straighten out our moral confusion and conflict?

The whole passage started significantly with the duty of love. This may appear to be a strange juxtaposition of utterly dissimilar elements, if we think of duty in Wordsworth's words as the 'Stern daughter of the voice of God'. But the emphasis here is that where there is love, the fulfilment of responsibilities is natural and joyous and warm-hearted.

And the Catechism follows up this analysis with equally sound advice: 'My good child, know this, that thou art not able to do these things of thyself . . . without God's special grace, which thou must learn at all times to call for by diligent prayer.' And the Lord's Prayer follows, with all its warmth and confidence.

3 The people next door

The parable of Jesus was given to a comparatively close-knit and static society. Men knew their neighbours, whether or not they acknowledged their responsibility towards them. This is not so today. Ours is a problem of contiguity coupled with anonymity. Continents, nations and races are crowded too close for comfort. It is significant that as peoples move into ever larger units of association and control, they react by demanding devolution and independence. Here is one of the roots of the nationalism which has spread so remarkably since 1945 in many parts of the world.

'Anonymity and contiguity' are the problems of the individual too. Social changes and constant movements of population make it difficult for men to achieve neighbourliness. Those who live near a man or work alongside him are his neighbours in material terms but not necessarily in fellowship and mutual support. When he falls into a difficult situation he feels helpless. The 'nuclear family' can be a human unit too lacking in resources in an emergency.

The Church has to recognise this situation and do what it can to help people in it. This is a very practical kind of Christianity to which Christians are being called. It does not mean an interfering intrusion into private lives. It means the open-door church in the household, as the New Testament describes it, sensitive and imaginative, going out to meet people where they are, making clear its willingness to help in any emergency . . . and not 'only waiting to be asked'. We are all instinctively reluctant to ask for help from a stranger— but Christians ought not to be strangers to the people among whom they live. For Christians need their neighbours, as much as their neighbours may need them. And where there is already a sense of mutual awareness and a felling of belonging, then the giving and the receiving can happen. The Samaritan did not wait to be asked to help someone whose only claim upon him was that he was a fellow human being—and therefore his neighbour.

CHRIST IN ACTION TODAY

Case for the defence

To the world, the sinner is more interesting than the saint and sin more newsworthy than virtue. That may be why popular opinion tends to regard the Prodigal Son as the hero of one of the best known of all Christ's parables. It has also persistently condemned the Elder as the villain, censorious over his brother's faults and hostile to his being accepted back into the fold.

We ought to get the facts straight. So we start with the reason why Jesus told this story. He did it to make clear to the Jews that their heavenly Father really cared about heathens and the sinners. If they repented, he was willing to welcome them back. The real hero of the parable is the Father.

1 *The faithful son*

In telling this parable, Jesus did not ignore the faithfulness of the Jews through the centuries. The case for the older son is presented sympathetically. If one imagines him telling the story in his own words, he might have said something like this:

'My father had always been indulgent to my young brother even though he never pulled his weight in the farm work. When the lad got restless and insisted on going out to see the world, my father gave in to him. That meant crippling the farm by realising half the capital. He went off and we didn't hear from him for years. Every day, my father looked out for him. He got more and more worried, particularly when we heard about the famine.

Then my brother came home, penniless and hungry. Knowing him, I felt sure he had only returned when he had spent everything. But you should have seen the fuss the old man made. Out came the best robe and the soft shoes and the ring— just like the treatment a distinguished visitor would get. The fatted calf was slaughtered. There was a party with music and dancing. I heard it all as I came back hot and tired after a day in the fields.

Well, I refused to go in. My father came out and asked me to join in. But I was too angry. I told my father straight. After all I'd served him obediently and faithfully all these years. I'd never been offered a chance to have a party with my friends. And now this ne'er-do-well turned up after a life of waste and self-indulgence, to be welcome and honoured. It just wasn't fair.

My father didn't deny this. He said just two things. One was to say that he never forgot that I was his son, who was always with him. So he did appreciate me after all. The other was to make the point that this was after all my own brother come back as if from the dead.

So what could I do?

What would you have done?'

2 No easy answer

There is no happy ending to the parable for Jesus did not say what the elder brother did eventually. As was so often the case, our Lord stated a principle without detailing the practice. The principle had to be worked out later. This was to cause great difficulty to the early Church, when Gentiles from the heathen world became Christians. It is impossible for us to appreciate how deep-rooted was the instinctive antipathy towards the heathen which the Jewish Christians had inherited. They disliked their religions, their morals and their eating habits. It became an important element in Paul's distinctive contribution to Christianity to work out a system of ethics which would bridge the gap. He tried to convey the best of the Jewish-Christian tradition in terms relevant to Gentile life. Yet as the Church in Jerusalem declined through persecution, dispersion and poverty, the surviving Jewish Christians there must have heard with mixed feelings about the spread of Christianity among the Gentiles.

The tension between the Prodigal and the Elder Brother recurred in the Church itself. Sometimes the hostility came from the conservatives, sometimes from those who saw themselves as the progressives. We glimpse this situation in the Colossian Epistle. There were those who claimed to possess a new and superior wisdom. The Gnostics of the second century professed to an exclusive knowledge of the truth and for a time were a serious menace to the Church. But there were other non-theological factors in the divisions of Christendom—questions of discipline, organisation, politics, nationalism, colour and race. What Christians have had in common in their allegiance to Christ has been forgotten when they have emphasised the points of difference. It has been all too easy for the Prodigal radical to denounce the Elder Brother as reactionary and for the latter to condemn his brother as irresponsible and destructive. And each has claimed to be the true son of the Father. We say that it is impossible to achieve the Brotherhood of Man until they recognise the Fatherhood of God. And this applies in the Church as well as in the world. For our common obedience to Christ, our deep need of each other as Christians, our responsibility to stand together for truth and love—these are far more important than our diversities of tradition or churchmanship or structure. We are in a time of crisis, and crisis means both danger and opportunity— to be faced by Christians who are together in Christ, brothers who have one Father.

3 *He came to himself*

As we have pointed out, there is no happy ending to this parable. But it is significant that Luke puts it in the context of the recovery of the lost. This is the theme of chapter 15 of this Gospel, with the three parables about the lost sheep, the lost coin and the lost son. Each of them is a parable with the note of joy. In the third, Jesus used a telling phrase about the Prodigal's change of heart: 'He came to himself.' His initial motive for returning home was not particularly noble. He merely remembered that even the servants back at home were better off than he was. Nevertheless the crux of the matter was his willingness to admit that he had been wrong. One can hope that the Elder Brother similarly 'came to himself'.

Jesus was teaching that when men came to themselves, they would discover their true identity as the sons of God and as brothers together. This concept of sonship was the key to the Kingdom. Men thought of it in terms of empire and power. Jesus meant by it the kingship of God in which they discovered their relationship with the Father. So the lost were found.

The recovery of the lost is always central to the purpose of the Gospel. There are no limits to its range. We forget this if we think of the Church as a kind of ambulance service confined only to the more obvious casualties of modern life. For the lost also include many who appear to have found themselves, all too satisfactorily. They have achieved material success and power and status. They consider themselves to be too sophisticated and civilised to have any need of the church or even of God. Yet they can constitute a problem for themselves and for others if behind the facade of achievement there is a kind of emptiness of soul. Something seems to have been lost on the way. Maybe this is the real self, the true identity, which the Prodigal discovered at a time of crisis. Having found it, he had the good sense to realise where he had gone wrong and to return to where he belonged.

This is a parable of realistic optimism with a message of particular relevance to our own situation. Man's view of himself is a curious mixture of pride and despair—proud of his material achievements, he despairs of human nature. He has a little confidence in others as he has in himself. Yet he can be capable of kindness and unselfishness, of loyalty and commitment, of courage and self-sacrifice. For this is his true nature. It is from this that he can respond to the needs of others with whom he identifies himself and to whom he gives love in the deepest sense of the word. Then he is behaving as man 'made in the image of God' and that which was lost had been found. And so the rediscovery of God's answer to the age-old question, 'What is man?' is what Christianity must offer to God's world today, with faith and with compassion.

CHRIST IN ACTION TODAY

The paradox of pain

The incident of Caesarea Philippi is often seen as a watershed in Christ's training of his disciples. After many months of journeying together, he suddenly asked them what public opinion said about him. They replied that people thought of him as John the Baptist or Elijah or one of the other prophets.

Then Jesus asked them a second question: 'But who do you say that I am?' Peter answered for them all: 'You are the Messiah.' It is not easy for us to appreciate just how great was the leap of faith and insight which lay behind this statement.

Then immediately Jesus began to disclose to the disciples the nature of the way that lay ahead, a way of suffering and death and resurrection. Peter's reaction was to say straightway: 'God forbid this shall happen to you!' For this, Jesus sternly rebuked him, even to the extent of commanding, 'Get thee behind me, Satan! You are a hindrance to me, for you are not on the side of God but on that of men.' Peter had acknowledged Jesus as Messiah, but he was unwilling to see him as the one who would redeem only through suffering and death.

1 *The power of pain*

Peter was only giving way to a very natural human reaction, that of allowing the prospect of pain to dominate one's response in a critical situation. The fear of pain is one of the greatest influences on human conduct. It may be more powerful than the desire for pleasure in affecting our decisions and choices. Much of our behaviour is not consciously thought out. It tends to be a matter of routine and habit of mind, however much we think of ourselves as having definite aims and objectives. We are moved to respond to stimuli from outside and from inside ourselves, largely under the influence of our emotions. But both in the long term and in the short term, the fear of pain can drive out every other consideration, suppressing conscience and over-riding our love for others.

This factor seems to have become increasingly significant in recent years. Pain tends to be regarded as the worst of all evils. There has been a phenomenal rise in the use of tranquilisers and drugs to alleviate pain and stress. No one would deny the benefit which these bring to vast numbers of sufferers although there is some evidence that too easy a recourse to them can lead to addiction, in many cases. Any merit attributable to patient endurance tends to be discounted.

Our attitude to the pain of others is curiously ambivalent.

On the good side, this generation can claim to be more aware of the sufferings of other people throughout the world particularly as regards the effects of natural disasters. We are also more sensitive than were our forefathers to the sufferings caused by the contemporary way of life, for example, through bad housing and unemployment. And we are more concerned about cruelty to animals.

But on the other side, we have to admit that in relationships with other people, our individualism and self-concern often leads us to cause them pain with hardly a qualm. This is as evident in the group-conflicts of industrialised societies as it is in the breakdown of family life with its rising tide of cruelty and desertion. Pain becomes something which others must put up with, even if for oneself it is seen as an evil to be avoided at all costs.

2 The value of pain

Yet pain is one of nature's most powerful and important forms of protecting life. If we never felt it, we should not know when we were in danger of being harmed by physical breakdown or even of being burnt by fire.

In the broader context of suffering, the acceptance of pain can play its part in achievement. Much of the progress of humanity has been attributable to people who were prepared to accept suffering for themselves in the course of scientific research—Marie Curie is an outstanding example. The same is true of many pioneers in the arts, in the defence of human rights, in political or religious emancipation. Believing as they did in the rightness of their cause, they were prepared to pay the price it involved. But this was because they accepted their personal obligation to the truth and did not leave it to others to achieve their objective. When, however, men come to expect the State to fulfill all such responsibility, then their readiness to make their personal contribution diminishes. We criticise the young for taking this attitude but they have only caught it from their elders. For we want love without pain, success without suffering, and reward without sacrifice.

3 Pain and faith

Shakespeare wrote:

> 'There was never yet a philosopher
> That could endure the toothache patiently.'

And that is true for Christians and non-Christians alike! Yet many of us have been privileged to know people who have been able to endure pain with amazing fortitude. They have been more concerned about the sufferings of others than of themselves. Any hospital ward will show instances of this. There it becomes evident that differences between such reactions of patients seem to depend less on the nature of their physical trouble, than on their inner response to it. What seems to matter is not condition but character.

This is reflected in the New Testament. As Stephen was being stoned to death in agony, he could still pray for the forgiveness of his enemies. His example had a marked effect on Saul of Tarsus. Later as the Apostle Paul, he could tell the Colossians that he rejoiced in his own sufferings for their sakes. He puts suffering into a theological context: 'In my flesh I complete what is lacking in Christ's afflictions for the sake of his body, that is, the Church.' The Christians are in mystical union with Christ so what Paul endures for the sake of others can be called Christ's sufferings. This takes us back through the centuries to the Suffering Servant of Isaiah and its great revelation that man is at his highest when suffering vicariously. This is redemptive love. This is pain redeeming the world with no thought of self. We experience this for ourselves when we love someone to the utmost. When he or she suffers, we long to suffer instead. In marriage or parenthood or deep friendship, we would sacrifice ourselves willingly—that is, literally, with the whole will. Then as Christ promised, by losing ourselves, we find ourselves.

Nevertheless it is hard to accept this as a price which may have to be paid for our membership in Christ. And it has always been so. As the first Epistle of Peter showed, it was not easy for Christians in northern Asia Minor to face persecution for their faith. In the previous century Jews had known savage oppression. But the persecutions which Christians encountered must have been to them a new and formidable test of their religion. Many fell away under great trials but sufficient remained faithful for the Church to continue. As Tertullian wrote: 'The blood of the martyrs is the seed of the Church.' They could only endure great suffering because of their deep sense of obedience to what they believed to be the will of God.

The call to witness in suffering came as a shock to many early Christians, so it does to the Church in this century. The optimism of the past about the unhampered spread of the Gospel has been shattered by events. There is oppression in many countries where religious 'toleration' is in effect intimidation. Totalitarian regimes try to destroy Christianity by direct attack or by ridicule. They have no illusions about its challenge to their ideologies and practices. Even in the western democracies the state tries increasingly to restrict the freedom of Christianity and to limit its scope for direct service to the community. The record of this century shows how important it is for the Church to recognise the situations and moments when direct confrontation is the only way of witnessing to truth, and to realise that the Cross is the sign of pain endured for God's sake, and man's. It is only then that the Cross can become also the sign of victory for the Church as it was for her Lord.

CHRIST IN ACTION TODAY

They walk alone

After the service, the woman said to the clergyman: 'I wonder why you pray so often for families and so rarely for those of us who have no families. Yet at least a quarter of the congregation must be loners like me.'

The vicar recognised that she was right. He had been

accustomed to country parishes where everybody seemed to know everybody. He had not realised how many of the people in his 'bed-sitter' district of the city, lived alone and were strangers to each other.

It was one of those areas where the problem of loneliness is acute. This is one consequence of what Simone Weil called 'the malaise of uprootedness'. In this century millions have moved from small communities into the concrete jungles of the inner-city or to the vast sprawls of housing estates. We are recognising belatedly that the high-rise tower blocks of flats put up in the 1950s and 1960s create more problems than they solve. Those problems are particularly serious in respect of the isolation of individuals and families.

To some, this does not matter too much. They can cope with solitariness. If they want to do so, they have little difficulty in establishing contact with other people and making meaningful relationships. But many others cannot deal with this situation by themselves. They withdraw from the outside world and sometimes break under the strain, so that loneliness becomes one of the major causes of suicide. 'Keeping myself to myself' used to be regarded as merely a rather silly form of pride. Now it has become almost a disease. Many doctors, solicitors and others who deal with people on an individual basis find themselves having to go beyond their professional functions to cope with what one might call a pastoral situation which is as much as anything one of desperate loneliness.

1 Christ and the lonely ones

Jesus was acutely sensitive to this problem. Many of the people he collected around him were 'loners'. Some, like Mary Magdalene, were the rejects of their society. Others, like Zacchaeus and the rich young man, were individuals who were restless and ill at ease despite their apparent prosperity. Many of his most moving parables were about individuals. In his mission he gave himself to folk one by one, from the woman of Samaria to Nicodemus. To Jesus, no person was a type and no situation was a case. He was able to collect his disciples as individuals, in most instances, and weld them into a fellowship. Indeed, fulfilling the promise of Psalm 68.6, the Son of God was 'setting the solitary in families'. The New Testament shows how this continued and the Epistles frequently refer to 'the church in the household'. The family was the centre for worship and evangelism. Its hospitality could be counted on for welcome to the stranger and to the itinerant ministry of men like Paul as he moved around the eastern Mediterranean.

2 *The one and the many*

But the New Testament knows nothing of individualistic Christianity, of the kind which might claim 'I'm a Christian although I don't got to church, and I'm just as good as those who do.' Nor does it envisage the 'Here am I, send him' type who comes to worship but refuses to take any part in the rest of the fellowship and service of the church.

The Church recognised that there are differences of approach to religion. One may need quiet and solitude in the devotional life. Another may respond heartily and willingly to a life of active fellowship. What the Church asks of its members is essentially *voluntary* service and participation.

Nevertheless, as Paul insisted, the Body of Christ is a living organism like a human body, of which no part has the right to say 'I have no need of thee' to its fellow members. He saw Christianity as involving a responsible relationship of mutal interdependence between people united in faith and love and action for God. This is the meaning of membership in Christ which is made explicit in baptism, confirmation and Holy Communion.

But what he says about the statement 'I have no need of thee' has implications for the Church itself in its ministry to the individual in trouble. This means that a congregation might ask itself what it is doing for the person who has to cope with solitariness. The women who asked the question with which we began, put one aspect of the problem. Another was illustrated by the remark of a widow: 'When my husband was alive we went everywhere together and we had many friends in the church. After he died, I was on my own and people just didn't seem to want to know . . . '

At times a newcomer to a congregation receives a welcome which is short-lived and superficial and he can feel frozen out by the 'in-groups'. It has to be admitted also that people who enjoy a happy life in their own homes can be incapable of understanding, and even listening sympathetically, to the problems of others whose experience of life has been less fortunate than their own. Asked why he had not sought help from his local church, a man who had been in serious difficulties said: 'They wouldn't understand. The church is all right for people who find it easy to be good, not for people with problems like mine.'

There might have been in this man's situation some justification for this sweeping condemnation. It may be doubted, however, whether any one really finds it 'easy to be good' or is without personal problems. At a recent conference of Christians the speaker asked his audience if any of them was personally concerned about a problem of broken marriage or a family under similar stress within the range of his or her immediate relatives or friends. Amost every one of his audience frankly acknowledged this to be the case. In fact one of the merits of recent developments in church life has been a greater openness in sharing personal experience—both of problems of living the Christian life in the contemporary context, and of the grace of God in dealing with them. Christians who come to terms with their own situation as individuals are better able to be of help to others, particularly those who find it hard to walk the way of loneliness. But it must be recognised that often they are in need of expert help beyond the capacity of most of us, whether spiritual or psychological. This has certainly been the experience of organisations such as the Samaritans.

But at least we can begin by being alert to the needs of others, understanding their situations and caring about them as human beings. The cry of many in distress is that nobody seems to care—not even God. Jesus showed that the Father cared by the way he himself did so. In the Sermon on the

Mount (Matthew 6.25-33) he insisted that every single person matters to God as Father and so need not feel anxiety or isolation. This divine love he himself conveyed in his sensitivity and ministry to individuals. Because men could believe in him, they could believe in God.

If we think of Christianity as the imitation of Christ, then we have to dare to ask if the people whom we have been talking about can believe in *us*, and so be helped to believe in God. It is not enough to be content with acts of charity or a readiness to be of service if only people would ask for it. The so-called 'silent Christian presence' is not enough. It has to be sustained by service to the point of self-sacrifice, by witness sometimes to the point of challenge, by illumination of the real situation of the person in trouble not least in respect of the potential of God's love to deal with it. For the caring of Christ was a kind of evangelism which asked for the response of faith. And the problem of loneliness is not only one of isolation without love. It is also one of living without faith—in oneself, in other people and in God. This is the faith which those who have it are under obedience to share with those who don't. It is not something which any Christian has the right to keep to himself.

CHRIST IN ACTION TODAY

Gospel for Bank Holiday

Millions who enjoy a Bank Holiday are not likely to know whom they have to thank for it. He was a Victorian philanthropist, John Lubbock, a man of many parts. This banker, author and politician, was also a scientist who became a Fellow of the Royal Society. As a Member of Parliament, he secured the passage of two Acts of Parliament which made an enormous difference to the lives of working people. One was the Early Closing Act of 1904. The other, passed in 1871, was the Bank Holidays Act.

Lubbock was deeply concerned about the needs of the working classes, their long hours of work and the slum conditions in which many of them lived. He believed that a holiday was their right as well as their need. He refused to endorse the theory that leisure was the privilege of the fortunate minority or to support the idea that work was sacred and an end in itself. He was implicitly putting to the society of his day a question which lies behind modern industrial welfare and the labour relations. This is not so much 'What is the work which has to be done?' as 'Who is the man doing the work?'

One may be permitted to wonder what John Lubbock might have thought of some aspects of the Bank Holiday today—the fantastic congestion of public and private transport, the high death-toll on the roads, the Battle of the Beaches, and the development of sporting activities which draw millions as spectators. He would however have appreciated that difficulties were bound to arise when multitudes of people do the same things at the same time. He would probably have been very much in favour of staggered holidays. But his chief concern was that people should have opportunities for recreation as well as recreation.

1 Holy days and holidays

Of course the idea of holidays was not new in the nineteenth century. Long before Christianity came, there were great festivals which were usually connected with the annual cycle of nature and its seasons. Many of these were taken over by the Church and linked with saints' days or festivals like Christmas and Easter. There were two sides to such events. One was religious in that they emphasised man's dependence on the grace of God. The other was social. The whole community came together in corporate activities, secular as well as religious, including processions and fairs and markets. Some of these secular commemorations survive to this day. Others have left behind customs and expressions of which the origin is almost forgotten. The word 'tawdry', for instance, goes back to the tawdry lace sold at the fair of St Audrey, or Etheldrida, patron saint of Ely.

So holidays, or holy-days as they were called until the fifteenth century, brought together the religious and the secular aspects of life in an experience of joyous re-creation of relationship and fellowship.

That, after all, was the purpose of the first holy day, the Sabbath. The fourth commandment is sometimes regarded as a negative one because of its prohibition of work. But its purpose was compassionate and humanitarian. It prescribed rest not only for the family of the household but also for the servants and for the stranger, who might be an alien. Even the working cattle were to be given rest.

However far back in the ancient history of the Semitic people lay the actual origins of the sabbath, the writers of the Bible regarded it as a day with a difference and one which gave meaning to the work of the rest of the week. After the Exile, the observance of the sabbath came to be one of the distinctive marks of the Jewish people. It is true that by our Lord's time the sabbath observance had become fenced around by a host of petty restrictions which bore hard upon the common people. Jesus had to recall his hearers to the fact that the sabbath had been made for man and not man for the sabbath. That did not mean that a man could do just what he liked with it in mere self-indulgence. For if Jesus appeared to break regulations of the sabbatarian code, he emphasised that it was in order that man should be able to fulfil the fundamental purpose of God underlying all the commandments.

2 The Lord's Day

At first Christians kept both the sabbath as well as the first day of the week which commemorated the Resurrection. Gradually as Christianity moved out into the Gentile world, the observance of the sabbath disappeared. Some aspects of its observance became transferred to the first day. But it must be remembered that many of the believers in the first and second centuries were slaves, compelled to do a full day's work on a

Sunday. When they met together for worship it would have to be very early in the morning. Then, as a historian records, 'They sang hymns to Christ as God' and celebrated the eucharist. What they did on that day made all the difference to the rest of the week. It was a day or renewal of fellowship. They took counsel together or received letters from other churches. Then they would return to their work with new strength and fresh vision.

Within the family of the church, the families worshipped together. This has been the tradition for centuries and it has been strengthened in this generation in Anglican churches, by the development of the parish communion as the main Sunday service, attended by children and adults of all ages. This is not without its problems. But one advantage is that children and young people can see worship as a normal adult pattern of behaviour, not as something which they leave behind with childhood. There is still truth in the saying that 'the family that prays together stays together'. Nevertheless it has to be faced that for many families Sunday is not really a day of unifying fellowship. The various members pursue their own interests and activities, and perhaps employment, outside the home. The increasing pressure of secularisation demands more facilities for entertainment even if this means that more people are compelled to work on a Sunday so that others may play. Sunday then becomes merely part of the week-end. It is not unreasonable to ask if this really meets human needs. Or did Jesus have something more profound in mind when he spoke of the sabbath as being made for man?

3 The holy day

We suggested at the outset that John Lubbock was implicitly asking a question as to who is the man engaged in his work. The same question can be asked about the man when he is not engaged in his work and what he really needs then. Most of us are aware that life can become a routine of busy-ness, of constant activity or dreary monotony. Our efforts to escape from this by seeking pleasure may do little to resolve our basic problem of coping with our weekday situation, of coming to terms with life and finding real happiness. Perhaps we need most to set apart a time which is essentially different from our ordinary experience—a time to think about life as a whole, a time for a deeper relationship with those we love, a time to renew the resources on which we draw unthinkingly every day. And those resources include, above all, the grace of God.

Throughout his ministry, Jesus was concerned to bring to everyone the gift of wholeness. That was why he healed on the sabbath in the face of the religious conventions of his time. He offers the same healing and the same wholeness today, in the face of the secular conventions of our time. He does this as the Saviour and as the Risen Lord. So to keep the Lord's day 'holy' is not only an act of obedience to God's will. It is also a realistic recognition of human need.

CHRIST IN ACTION TODAY

The real harvest

He had never lived in a rural area before becoming a country parson. He faced his first Harvest Festival there with some misgivings. It had been a bad summer and a worse autumn, with days of continuous rain. So he asked his churchwarden how people could be expected to sing songs of thanksgiving as if all were 'safely gathered in'. The old farmer replied: 'It wouldn't be a proper Festival without all the familiar hymns, just as usual. This harvest was bad. But last year's was good and maybe next year's will be too. You've got to take the long view, Rector.'

The following year friends from the city came to visit him. They said how lucky he was to have all the fruit and vegetables in his garden. 'How lucky!' He thought somewhat ruefully of the hours of work in the half-acre rectory garden, which had been put in by his wife and himself . . . and made no comment.

He had seen for himself two aspects of harvest—the long view and the view from behind the scenes. He remembered also the Harvest Festivals of war time. Then there was little enough to spare for bringing up as gifts. The U-boat menace was always in the background and the country was at times very near the edge of subsistence. Imports were brought in at the cost of many lives. It was impossible to be other than profoundly grateful for even the daily bread.

Seen in this light, the Harvest Festival is never a sentimental exercise irrelevant to a sophisticated society. It is a recall to reality.

1 *The seed and the soil*

In much of his teaching Jesus used realistic illustrations drawn from the agricultural life of Palestine. He had no illusions about the hard work involved in the constant battle against the vagaries of Nature. But in one of his most 'agricultural' parables he focussed upon the importance of the soil itself.

The parable of the Sower is recorded in Matthew, Mark and Luke. It was delivered to the multitude without explanation. Afterwards the disciples took Jesus aside. They asked what it meant and why indeed he taught in parables at all. To the latter question Jesus replied that parables were a test of insight and spiritual awareness. Then he explained the meaning of the parable in detail to the disciples as part of their preparation for their own mission. They were to learn from him never to be surprised by the failure or the success of the proclamation of the Gospel. For a crucial factor in determining the response to it would be the personality of the hearer. One man might listen without understanding a word of it. To him the Gospel would be like seed scattered on a well-worn path. Another would receive it with short-lived enthusiasm which would not survive tribulation or persecution. A third category would accept the truth, but it would be the good soil which bore a rich harvest. The seed would be the same in all four cases. Its harvest would differ according to the responsiveness of the soil.

2 The Gospel and the people

The modern Church is greatly concerned about the problem of communication, mainly in terms of content and method. But in this parable Jesus helps us to look at this problem as it affects people with whom the Church tries to communicate. We realise that the four categories persist in every generation. There are always the 'wayside' folk who believe themselves to have no need of religion. They might be annoyed to be told that they were not Christians, for they have equated Christianity with 'decent chapmanship'. They might claim never to have done any harm to anyone, but it would be doubtful if they have ever sought to do anyone any good.

The next two groups are equally ineffective, and their religion equally rootless. They begin well in enthusiastic membership of their church. But the world gets too much for them, when life becomes difficult or they are subjected to criticism and ridicule as Christians. Even when this does not happen, they may still prefer the 'broadmindedness' of the world to the 'straight and narrow way' of the Christian ethic. Secular priorities become their priorities. They may still keep up the appearance of being Christians but their religion bears no fruit in their lives.

The parable suggests that in all three examples, when people are like this, the preaching of the word is unable to change them. So Christ's disciples, in any age, must not be dismayed or angry when this kind of failure happens to them—as it did to Christ.

3 Christ the optimist

Faced with this sort of situation, the Christian may be tempted to despair. It would be more to the point if he were to try to consider what had made the soil so unresponsive. But Christ takes a completely different line. His parable is as realistic about success as it is about failure. He says that where there is a true and lasting response, the yield far outweighs the amount of seed scattered. He himself preached to multitudes, and left behind only eleven men and a handful of women. From them grew the Church which even today numbers one-third of the world's population. The parable is reminding us that what matters is not the size of the majority but the commitment of the minority and its capacity for growth and fruitfulness.

4. *By their fruits*

That the early Church took this message to heart is evident from the fact that almost every book in the New Testament stresses the importance of fruitfulness to the Christian life. This is not a demand for good works as objectives of human effort. Instead, it presents them as the outward and visible signs of an inward and spiritual grace—if one may borrow an expression from the Catechism. Paul says that the fruit of the Spirit is love, joy, peace, patience, kindness, goodness, faithfulness, gentleness and self-control. These are not abstract qualities of character. They flow naturally into action in all relationships. And it is by these fruits that, as Jesus promised, Christians shall be recognised.

So the parable comes full circle. Jesus started by talking about the outside world and its response or lack of response to the Gospel. But the message was a challenge to the disciples themselves, as it is to us to ask what our own response is like. This is the question which every Harvest Thanksgiving puts to every Christian. We may realise that it is calling us to be grateful for all that we have received from God and from other people. That is part of the realism for it asks us to express our gratitude 'not only with our lips but with our lives'.

But its message goes still deeper. For it would make us think about the harvest which we are producing in the lives of others. At times we may be inclined to take stock of ourselves and to ask what we have achieved with our life in terms of success or status or personal happiness. But what matters even more is what we have done for others, not least in helping them to find faith and hope and love in their own lives. We can never know how little or how great this has been. Perhaps fortunately, no man can read his own obituary! But at least we can know that it is the privilege and responsibility of every Christian to share in sowing the seed of the Gospel of the Kingdom—and to leave the results to God. The world regards productivity as essential to the survival of the economy. Christianity believes that spiritual productivity is essential to the survival of mankind. And Jesus expects it of everyone who bears the name of Christian.

CHRIST IN ACTION TODAY

War and peace

The annual commemoration of Remembrance Day and Battle of Britain Sunday, and comparable events in other countries, are always the subject of argument. The young may watch the parades and ceremonies with mystification. Some of their elders argue that these annual rituals revise old antagonism and stir up ancient enmity. Another contention is that they tend to glamorise war itself as noble and heroic, masking the fact that it is brutal and wasteful and can evoke the worst in human nature. There may be some substance in these points of view. But what really matters is whether or not, in the words of Deuteronomy, we 'remember all the way'.

'All the way' incorporates so many diverse experiences in wartime. One remembers the utter disbelief that this could possibly happen. There was the darkness of successive defeats, the nights of fear during air raids, the pain and suffering and bereavement and captivity, the inhumanity of man to man. There was the dishonesty and selfishness which shortages and insecurity could foster. But there was the other side, of patient endurance, of courage and self-sacrifice shown often by the most unlikely people, the comradeship and co-operation and inspired leadership. One effect of war was to bring out the best and the worst in human nature. There is some value in being reminded of this. The annual remembrance brings home to us what war does to people. It should also make us think more deeply about the way in which we drift into conflict at any level. For the roots of war are there at all times and there is no easy means of eradicating them.

1 Roots of war

It has been said that civilisations have been brought to ruin through one or other of three main causes—slavery, usury and war. Of these the effect of war is the most obvious, if its origins are the most complex. These have included economic pressures such as the failure of harvests at one end of a continent starting a chain reaction which brought invaders to batter at the gates of Rome. The battle for raw materials or the pressure of population can be other factors of importance.

There is a whole range of political pressures which can lead to war. National ambition can demand territory and status. Attention can be diverted from internal troubles by arousing hatred against neighbouring powers. The ruthless suppression of truth by propaganda is a ready tool for the demagogue and the power-hungry.

But the most important roots of war lie in men's minds. They are the area in which ideologies, nationalistic antagonism, racial antipathy or even religious prejudices arouse the hostility which leads to conflict. For war is essentially the expression of conflict of ideas. Its outcome does not prove whether those ideas are morally right or wrong. As to taking up arms against oppression and evil, men have argued for centuries whether such a situation constitutes a 'just war' or entitles the state to require the pacifist to share in its defence. Modern warfare has transformed the whole scene of argument by its indiscriminate impact upon the entire population of a nation, civilians and armed forces alike. In the last decade we have been compelled to recognise, through what has happened particularly in Africa and East Asia, the corruption which war can bring to simple and primitive people. We realise, too, that war is never final and peace is never absolute. At the end of a great conflict, the nations resolve to outlaw war and try to establish a federation to accomplish this. Yet they are never willing to surrender enough of their independence to achieve lasting peace. And so it goes on, while man cries 'O Lord, how long?'

2 *The answer of Christ*

Jesus said bluntly that it was out of the heart of man that war springs. This was not to deny the power of economic, political or ideological factors. Nor was he suggesting that his followers had no obligation to involve themselves in the problem. Yet one of the recurrent errors committed by Christians, like other people, has been that of ignoring the developments which have led to conflict and even standing aloof from them. They have tended to be apathetic and indifferent while others within their own nations have pursued policies which have resulted in war.

When Jesus blessed the peacemakers, he was not blessing the dewy-eyed optimism of the passively peaceful. He was praising those who try to make peace by their courageous stand for truth in the face of prejudice and misrepresentation. They try to understand the points of view of both sides, to make clear what lies behind their attitudes, to illuminate what they have in common as well as what divides them. Often the peacemakers get the worst of the situation. They are suspect to both parties in conflicts over political rights, national ambitions and racial antagonism. They are pressed by each to say that God is on their side. Refusal to do so brings the accusation of treachery, partisanship or, at best, over-idealism. Yet in fact what the mediator is attempting is to hold humanity to the true course from which war is an unnatural and sinful aberration.

3 *A question of perspective*

What happens on the world scene is the projection of what happens in the microcosm of the individual's own life. The conquest of war has to begin there. Our instincts drive us to give the highest priority to self-preservation and that can lead us to aggression when we feel ourselves to be threatened—

whether that threat is real or imaginary. The same is true of another area of instinctive behaviour, that of sex and the family. When we identify ourselves with the needs of the group, community, class, nation or race to which we belong, then our herd-instinct can also lead us to a combative reaction to danger. We may think we are acting rationally and responsibly when in fact our instincts are the real driving force. So the first step has to be one of 'Stop, Look and Listen'—to what is happening inside ourselves. We may then realise that our real hostility is towards something far deeper than the external stimulus of it. Our overt act of aggression may satisfy our need for action, but it will do little to deal with the real tension, within ourselves. It is there that what John described as 'fear' has to be replaced by love. This did not mean a mere sentimentality or a passive pretence of good will. He thought of love as an attitude of the whole personality. It starts from the inner security of knowing oneself to be loved by God and therefore being able to trust him. That confidence enables one to resist the pressures and threats of circumstances. It produces also the readiness to see others as they really are, sharing a common humanity with all its strength and weaknesses. Love is not blind to their faults or to one's own. But it knows how to deal with them by God's grace. For peace in the soul, as in relationships and in the world depends on putting life into its true perspective—seeing it in the dimension of God's power and God's purpose and God's love. For it is the Father who is the ultimate peacemaker for all humanity.